Legal Handbook for Financial Planning in 2019

For Middle Income and Upper-Middle Income Persons and Households

Allen Buckley

Forward

Suze Orman has preached to the masses about personal finances. The wealthy arm themselves with CPAs, attorneys and certified financial planners. There are few who offer financial planning aid to help middle and upper middle income persons and households—those making from $75,000 to $400,000 per year. This book, published in 2019, is designed to help this group.

This book does not explain how to invest. Its aim is to explain the federal and general states' legal systems as they relate to personal finances.

As noted in the first chapter, things will change, so the reader needs to realize that while this book's content is believed to be accurate in 2019, many of the laws discussed will change in the future. Thus, using it for analysis after 2019 is risky. While using it in 2019, care should be taken to realize that federal and state laws and regulations are very complex. The book provides a general overview of major laws impacting a large segment of the U.S. population. Some exceptions, etc. might not be covered. Individual research should be undertaken with respect to every significant transaction to ensure the desired (or presumed) results will be obtained.

Finally, Chapter 11 provides a summary of the major provisions of the federal entitlements system. While this material is dry (to say the least), a person not knowledgeable about these matters would likely find the rest of the materials in the book much easier to understand if Chapter 11's materials are first read. <u>Note</u>: In some places throughout this book, reference is made to Georgia law. This is so because the author resides in Georgia. Different laws exist in each of the fifty states.

ISBN: 9781091578821

Table of Contents

Chapter 1

A Complex and Ever-Changing System

The goal of this book is to give individuals and households making $75,000 to $400,000 in 2019 the building blocks to effectively plan to protect assets and minimize expense. This chapter summarizes the system that needs to be considered, in light of the financial standing of the U.S. The considerations summarized in this chapter make planning for the future *extremely difficult*.

Disclosure: Some of the material in this book is *flat-out boring*. It is the nature of the beast. I've tried to put things in simple understandable terms. If you understand the materials in this book, you'll have a solid knowledge of the financial system impacting U.S. residents.

In Chapter 12, decision-making is discussed. It involves deciding what variable factors (e.g. taxes) are potentially relevant to a decision, and then doing analysis considering those factors. How many factors will be relevant will turn on one's personal situation. For example, for a household with one self-employed person, making over $100,000 of income, and one or more kids in college or soon on their way thereto, taxes, Obamacare and federal financial aid for college will ordinarily be the relevant factors. Often, two factors will be relevant. You can then re-read the pertinent parts of chapters relevant thereto before doing analysis.

Between the federal and state legal, tax and entitlements systems, and all accompanying regulation, financial planning in the U.S. is now more difficult than it ever was in the past. Looking for some comfort? It will likely be more difficult in the future.

While tax and investment planning have been common and necessary in the U.S. for a long time, recent expansion of entitlements to cover middle and even upper middle income persons and households has made prudent decision-making more difficult. Historically, it has been commonplace to use the existing legal and tax systems to plan for the future. However, for the reasons outlined below, using the current systems probably is not reasonable. (The obvious question becomes: What can be used?)

On their own, many of the components of the federal and states' legal, tax and regulatory systems are not so bad. It's when they are put together that things become very complex. Understanding them requires time and thought. Nevertheless, the materials that follow in this book will hopefully supply you with information that can be used to help minimize financial harm and supply personal gain.

Consider the (significantly modified in 2017) federal tax system. For income, it requires an analysis of whether a thing is income and, if so, when it is income, what type of income it is, and its amount. Deductions pose similar complexities, along with the additional need to determine whether "capitalization" is required. (Capitalization means treating a thing purchased as an asset that produces benefits over two or more years, thus ordinarily requiring that the asset be depreciated for tax purposes over years using a statutorily-specified method and life.) Obamacare's addition of a 3.8 percent tax on investment income, and its accompanying hundreds of pages of regulations, necessitate an additional accounting system.

The costs to comply with the U.S. tax system are staggering. A June 2016 report by the Scott A. Hodge of *The Tax Foundation* titled "The Compliance Costs of IRS Regulations" reported that compliance costs in 2016 were

$409 billion, and required 8.9 billion hours. Many are realizing that the system's complexity is a drag on the economy that needs to be greatly reduced. As explained in Chapter 5, the recently enacted Tax Cuts and Jobs Act of 2017 (TCJA) increased complexity in some ways and decreased it in some ways.

Prior to 1913, the federal income tax did not exist. And, when the federal income tax first started, it applied only to wealthier Americans. Obviously, it has grown. In recent years, total federal revenue collections have ordinarily been in the range of 16-20 percent of U.S. Gross Domestic Product (i.e. GDP—the annual output of goods and services). Many economists believe growth of taxes beyond the 20 percent range stifles economic growth.

Prior to 1935, Social Security did not exist. Today, it is the federal government's most costly program in terms of amounts paid—anticipated to cost roughly $1 trillion dollars (i.e. $1,000,000,000,000) in 2019. It is largely funded by payroll taxes.

Prior to 1965, Medicare and Medicaid did not exist. Together, their costs now exceed those of Social Security, and they are expected to grow tremendously in the coming years.

Over time, federal entitlements have, as an almost absolute rule, only grown. However, based on the anticipated growth of federal spending outlined in the following chart, things will change.

Figure 1-8.

Federal Debt Held by the Public

Percentage of Gross Domestic Product

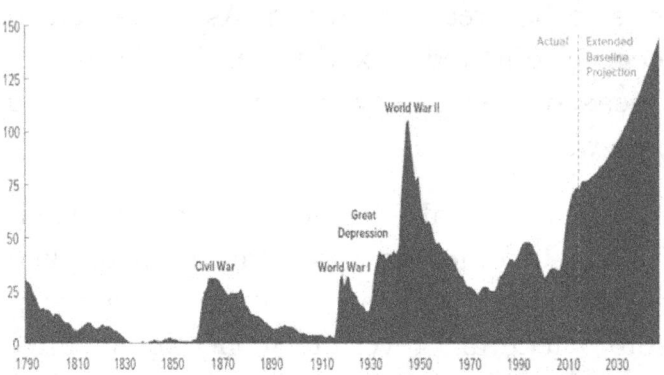

High and rising federal debt would reduce national saving and income in the long term; increase the government's interest payments, thereby putting more pressure on the rest of the budget; limit lawmakers' ability to respond to unforeseen events; and increase the likelihood of a fiscal crisis.

Source: Congressional Budget Office. For details about the sources of data used for past debt held by the public, see Congressional Budget Office, *Historical Data on Federal Debt Held by the Public* (July 2010), www.cbo.gov/publication/21728.

The extended baseline generally reflects current law, following CBO's 10-year baseline budget projections through 2027 and then extending most of the concepts underlying those baseline projections for the rest of the long-term projection period (in this case, through 2047).

If the debt growth anticipated in the above chart comes to fruition, the United States is finished. The system likely reaches a breaking point within 20-25 years. Before then, on our nation's current path, things will get difficult as federal borrowing increases to cover the entitlements. Simultaneously, other democracies will experience the same baby boomer financial problems. Add in the pension and post-retirement health care funding problems of state and local governments (which are substantial—many mid-size and large cities have already filed bankruptcy largely in connection therewith—states do not have this option), and you have a very different U.S. than what has been known since World War II.

The following chart shows how ordinary federal "government" spending has basically held the line or even decreased in recent years, while entitlements' spending has grown substantially:

4

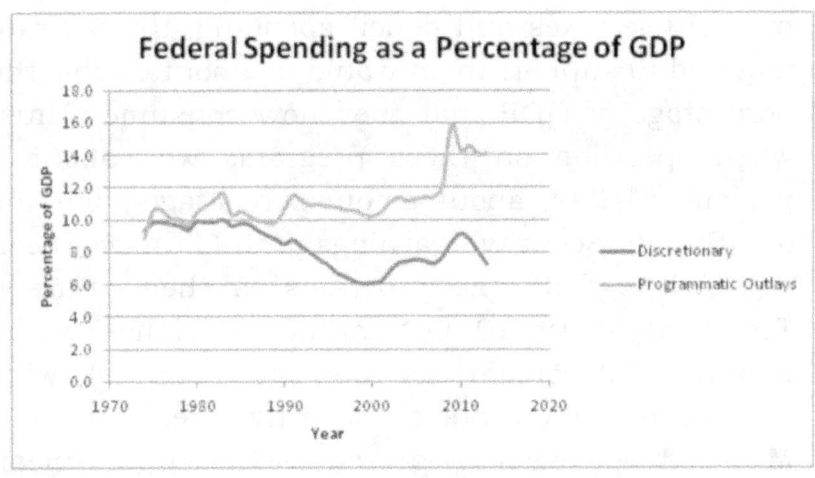

Federal Spending as a Percentage of GDP

As explained in the chart, entitlements (Programmatic Outlays above) are the increased spending culprit. Either they will be reduced or the federal government will likely collapse. The depth of the problem was explained in 2007 (i.e. before the Great Recession) by the head of the federal government's auditor, the Government Accountability Office (GAO), when he (David Walker) said: "GAO's current long-term simulations continue to show ever larger deficits resulting in a federal tax burden that ultimately spirals out of control."

In August 2010, then Joint Chiefs of Staff head Admiral Mike Mullen said: "The most significant threat to our national security is our debt."

A 2014 book by former Assistant Deputy Secretary of the Treasury economist C. Eugene Steuerle, titled *Dead Men Ruling*, provides the following on page 74:

> Social Security, Medicare, and Medicaid (close to half of which goes toward long-term care) dominate the modern history of domestic government . . . Were all three of these programs fully financed by simple, transparent taxes such as the Social Security payroll tax, rather than financed

by multiple taxes and deficit spending, the tax rate required to support them would be about double the percentage of GDP that they now consume. Thus, when spending on these programs was about 2 percent of GDP, about a four-percentage-point tax on Social Security earnings would have been required to fund the programs in their entirety. Today, at about 10 percent of GDP, they would require a 20 percent tax rate. Projections showing that spending on Social Security, Medicare, and Medicaid will reach 20 percent of GDP would mean about a 40 percent tax rate *for these programs alone.*

On page 83, Mr. Steuerle notes the possible outcome at some point in time:

Nations that face exploding debt levels or the kind of problems outlined above [relating the U.S.'s financial problems] often refuse to pay their debts and declare bankruptcy. Because so many nations depend on the U.S. dollar to stabilize world markets, a U.S. default could prompt not just a U.S. crisis, but a global depression. U.S. government bonds and bills have long served as the go-to safety vehicle for investors. A U.S. dollar default would shake the global economy to its core because it would signal that U.S. bonds and bills are no longer the rock-solid investments on which investors around the world have long relied.

In December 2010, The National Commission on Fiscal Responsibility and Reform (the Bowles-Simpson commission) issued its much anticipated report. In its preamble, the report provided:

Our challenge is clear and inescapable: America cannot be great if we go broke. Our businesses will not be able to grow and create jobs, and our workers will not be able to compete successfully for jobs of the future without a plan to get this crushing debt off our backs. . . . Over the course of deliberations, the urgency of our mission has become all the more apparent. . . . If the U.S. does not put its house in order, the reckoning will be sure and the devastation severe.

In The Mission segment of the Bowles-Simpson Report, the following is stated: "By 2025 revenue will be able to finance only interest payments, Medicare, Medicaid and Social Security."

Having all the money in the world does little or no good if the system collapses.

If a collapse or worldwide depression occurred with the U.S. heavily in debt, the stock market would certainly collapse as well. With it, it would take retirement accounts. That's potentially catastrophic.

In recent years, the U.S. has experienced nothing but low interest rates. And, if more traditional rates applied, the federal government could easily become unhinged sooner rather than later. With (in early 2019) roughly $16 trillion of federal public debt, and $3.3 trillion of federal revenue in 2018, a more traditional interest rate of five percent (5%) would necessitate annual interest costs of $800 billion—24 percent of total federal revenue. By 2047, the CBO anticipates total public debt to equal 150 percent of GDP. At 5 percent interest, over 40 percent of tax revenue would be needed to pay annual interest expense.

Congress is adept at increasing entitlements. However, it has virtually no experience at, and has shown virtually no appetite for, substantially decreasing entitlements. Such is the nature of a democracy (or a republic). You win by promising as much or more than the opposition, while taking the same or less.

In its Spring 2017 edition, *The International Economy* asked 37 economic and financial experts from around the world the following question: "Has the World Been Fitted with a Debt Straightjacket?" Most said yes, or essentially yes. A few said "absolutely not." Other answers were more muddled. Thomas Mayer, Founding Director of the Flossbach von Storch Research Institute, and former chief economist for Deutsche Bank, said:

> It seems Japan's experience of the last three decades has been replicated on a global scale. . . . As long as there is no exogenous shock to inflation, the fragile equilibrium will continue. Inflation has been very low on trend in Japan since the early 1990s and it has been low in other industrialized countries since the financial crisis of 2007. But the fragile equilibrium will break apart when inflation eventually rises. Then, central banks will be confronted with the choice of either raising interest rates at the risk of triggering a wave of defaults by over-indebted entities, or keeping rates low at the risk of loss of credibility and mass flight out of paper money. Having to choose between pestilence and cholera, they will most likely go for cholera and keep rates down. The consequence would be the long-awaited surge in inflation, which could turn into a collapse of the paper (or "fiat") money system.

Many of the other experts had somewhat similar views, although perhaps not as bold.

All Americans should be concerned about where things are headed. How do the federal finances tie into financial planning? The bottom line is: One way or another, *the system will change, and **it will change substantially**.* The difficult question becomes: How to plan for the future?

It is likely than entitlements eventually will be reduced to some degree, and the federal government will not collapse. But, along the way, there will be much angst. The incredibly complex tax system could, and very likely will, change substantially. For example, tax rates could rise substantially, to levels experienced in the 1940s to 1970s— when the highest rates were much higher than the current highest rate of 37 percent. In 1944, the highest rate was 94 percent; in 1953, it was 91 percent. Alternatively or additionally, a value-added tax (VAT) could be added to increase revenue. Virtually all industrialized nations except the U.S. have a VAT or a tax on retail sales.

Keeping these factors in mind, let's turn to an examination of what things are, and very likely will continue to be, favored under the federal legal system.

Chapter 2

Federally Favored Activities and Groups

With the nation's financial problems in mind, it is important to understand that certain activities and groups are generally favored by both the federal and states' legal systems. The following activities are currently favored. For the reasons given in Chapter 1, the law will change in many significant respects. However, it is likely that the more favored an activity currently is, the less of a "hit" it will take in the future as the tax system and entitlements systems experience reform.

Retirement Benefits. The most favored activity is saving for retirement through tax-qualified retirement plans such as 401(k) plans and IRAs. The benefits include:

- Except for a Roth account and subject to limits, an income tax deduction for contributions
- Potential tax credits for lower-income contributors (i.e. the Saver's credit—discussed in Chapter 5)
- Tax-free growth of assets and income thereon
- Assets generally excluded from the FAFSA (federal financial aid for college) calculations
- Assets generally protected from creditors in the event of bankruptcy, and often outside bankruptcy
- Assets generally protected from IRS collection activities
- Assets can be converted to an annuity to minimize or eliminate nursing home costs
- Distributions generally not required until age 70½ or even later (for most employed persons with respect to their employers' plans) — not required for Roth IRAs
- Assets excluded from food stamps eligibility calculations

- Roth account distributions ordinarily tax-free.

Following termination of employment, tax-qualified plan benefits held in employer plans can be "rolled over" tax-free to IRAs by individuals, thus permitting continued tax-free growth.

Owning a Home. Owning a home produces many benefits. Included in the benefits are:

- Income tax deductions for most home mortgage interest payments
- Much or all of the gain on sale is tax-free
- Exclusion from the FAFSA college financial aid calculations
- Generally exempt from IRS collection activities; reachable by creditors in bankruptcy to a limited degree (can vary substantially based on state law)
- General exemption from Medicaid nursing home calculations while living
- Exclusion from food stamps eligibility calculations.

While owning a home is a favored activity, the logic for tax-deductibility of home mortgage interest is suspect. Regarding subsidies for home ownership, the 2005 *President's Advisory Report of Federal Tax Reform* (created for President H.W. Bush) noted on page 72:

> Although the deduction for home mortgage interest is often justified on the grounds that it is necessary for promoting home ownership, it is unclear to what extent rates of home ownership depend on the subsidy. According to the Census Bureau, there are more than 123 million homes in America, with a home ownership rate of 69 percent. There are many countries that do not allow any home mortgage deductions for tax

purposes, including the United Kingdom, Canada, and Australia. The rate of home ownership in the United States is higher than that in some countries (approximately 66 percent in Canada), lower than that in others (approximately 70 percent in Australia), and comparable to that in still others (the United Kingdom). Thus, it appears that the level of subsidies provided in the United States may not be necessary to ensure high rates of home ownership.

So, as Congress (hopefully) looks for means of saving money, the home mortgage deduction will likely experience at least a reduction. The Tax Cuts and Jobs Act (of 2017) slightly reduced the mortgage deduction, and eliminated deductions for home equity loan interest.

Certain Work. With the very important exception of people who are at the upper end of the lower-income scale and people who have children in college, work generally is favored. Generally, cash flow to the household increases as cash income from work increases. The earned income tax credit is available only to workers who earn money. And work, or attempted work, generally is necessary for the nonelderly to receive food stamps. However, for households at the upper end of the lower income scale (e.g. a family of four making roughly $29,000 per year in 2014), making more money can potentially reduce lifestyle because of reduced eligibility for entitlements and refundable tax credits. Generally, a family of four making $29,000 per year that receives all available entitlements and tax credits does not experience an increase in lifestyle until income exceeds approximately $50,000 (as of 2014). Things have changed little since 2014. As noted in Chapter 7, making more money can result in less college aid.

Being in Need. As discussed further in Chapter 11, a tremendous amount of benefits are provided for people who are in need. As need decreases, entitlements decrease. One's lifestyle can diminish significantly due to loss of entitlements. Practically, the current system creates incentives for a large part of the population to "lay low" and stay in the income range that qualifies for the federal and state entitlements.

Debt. The U.S. system favors debt. Home mortgage debt interest generally is tax-deductible for income tax purposes. Whenever the Federal Reserve Bank engages in "quantitative easing," it is essentially printing money, thereby decreasing the value of each existing dollar. If one is a debtor and the value of the dollar decreases, debt substantively diminishes. Finally, debts reduce net worth and, as explained below, net worth generally is a significant factor in determining federal financial aid for college and entitlement to nursing home care.

Having Children. Tax credits exist for each child, as well as for college costs of children. Growing family size increases the amount of household income that can be received without losing eligibility for entitlements. The more children a family has, the more of certain entitlements the family is entitled to receive (e.g. food stamps). Minimizing the age differences between children maximizes the federal financial aid for college a family can receive.

Health Care. Generally speaking, health care provided by an employer is tax-free to the employee. Subject to potential reduction for Obamacare tax credits, self-employed persons, including partners in service partnerships and LLCs, can deduct the full cost of health insurance for income tax purposes. Also, if the coverage qualifies as a high deductible health plan described in Internal Revenue Code Section 220, then a health savings account (HSA) can be maintained that provides for tax-deductible contributions to it, tax-free growth of assets, and tax-free distributions as long as the distributions are used to pay for health care. The 2019 contribution limits for HSAs are $3,500 for single coverage and $7,000 for family coverage.

Gifting, Including Charitable Gifting. Gifts reduce net worth, and net worth generally is a determining factor for many entitlements, including federal financial aid for college and nursing home care. Subject to limits, charitable gifts ordinarily are tax-deductible.

Being Old. As the baby boomers continue to retire and become eligible for Medicare and Social Security, the political power of seniors (that has always been great) continues to grow. It is no secret that a very high percentage of seniors vote. They generally vote to protect their interests. It is in their interest that Medicare and Social Security, the two largest federal entitlement programs, continue to exist without cuts and even be expanded. Indeed, the Republicans expanded Medicare in 2004 by adding Part D.

As federal cuts are proposed, expect seniors as a group to flex their collective muscle. Organizations like AARP will act to protect them. However, in the end, for the federal government to endure, it is very likely that Medicare or Social Security (or both) will experience some cuts.

As government cuts (hopefully) eventually do take place over time, the things and groups described above will likely whether the storm better than other activities and groups. However, those lacking a solid basis for support, such as home mortgage subsidies, will likely see reduction and perhaps even elimination.

Chapter 3

Asset Protection

This chapter primarily covers means of protecting assets from creditors and other undesirable things.

The laws of many states prefer creditors. For example, Official Code of Georgia (O.C.G.A.) section 18-2-20, titled "Rights of Creditors to be Favored by the Courts," states: "The rights of creditors shall be favored by the courts; and every remedy and facility shall be afforded them to detect, defeat, and annul any effort to defraud them of their just rights." So much for justice being pure.

Fraudulent transfers can essentially be reversed, with the assets available to creditors of the transferor debtor.

State laws differ on exactly when a transfer is fraudulent. Georgia law provides (in O.C.G.A. section 18-2-74) that a transfer is fraudulent if made with the actual intent to hinder, delay or defraud any creditor, or without receiving equivalent value and the debtor either: (a) was about to engage in a transaction for which the remaining assets of the debtor would be unreasonably small in relation to the business or transaction; or (b) intended to incur, or believed or reasonably should have believed that he or she would incur, debts beyond his or her ability to pay as they became due. A transfer of assets that is made when the transferor is insolvent, or that makes the transferor insolvent, is a consideration in determining whether a conveyance is fraudulent. Insolvency generally means that liabilities exceed the value of assets.

Retirement Plans. Holding assets in a tax-qualified retirement plan such as a 401(k) plan or pension plan is virtually always the safest way to protect them. Individual retirement accounts (IRAs) are another excellent place to store assets.

Assets held in a tax-qualified retirement plan are protected from creditors of the employer/plan sponsor and the participant, both inside and outside bankruptcy of the employer/plan sponsor and the participant. An exception exists for the IRS, but the IRS ordinarily does not pursue retirement plan assets. However, the assets held in a nonqualified retirement plan (i.e. a retirement or deferred compensation plan or arrangement that does not meet the requirements of Internal Revenue Code section 401(a)) are not protected from creditors.

With respect to IRAs in bankruptcy, federal law protects all IRA rollover funds (i.e. funds transferred from tax-qualified plans) and IRA funds not sourced from a tax-qualified plan rollover to the extent of $1,283,025 in 2018 (which originally was $1,000,000 in 2005, but is indexed for inflation every three years). However, an inherited IRA's assets can be reached by the creditors of the IRA death beneficiary in a bankruptcy situation. Means of protecting inherited IRA assets through an IRA trust are discussed below. State law specifies IRA protection outside bankruptcy. Georgia law provides that assets of IRAs generally are protected from garnishment. Exceptions exist for alimony and child support.

Insurance. As thoroughly discussed in Chapter 4, operating a business through a corporation or a limited liability company (LLC) generally limits the amount of risk to the amount invested. Certain risks cannot be eliminated or reduced through use of a legal entity. For example, practicing law in any legal form of entity in

Georgia does not protect a lawyer from a malpractice claim. Insurance can be purchased to reduce risk.

Insurance is often the only practical way of reducing risk. The problem with insurance is you have to pay for it. And, if a claim is filed, the insurance company must honor it. If you have a dog that might bite someone, either insure against the risk or get rid of the dog.

Health insurance, whether it is from an employer, a private insurance company or the government, is virtually a must. Unfortunately, for many persons, the cost of coverage is very expensive. The downside of not having health insurance can potentially be catastrophic.

If rental property exists, it is best that it be owned through an LLC, and sufficient insurance exist. Owning the rental property personally and leasing it to the LLC, followed by rental of the property by the LLC to the tenant, is probably the best way to go from a legal protection perspective. However, it might not be best from a federal financial aid for college standpoint. In any event, sufficient coverage should exist with respect to the property. Also, umbrella liability coverage is often inexpensive, and it may protect against personal liability in the event of a successful "piercing of the corporate (or LLC) veil," as discussed elsewhere herein.

A business might have valuable operating assets, including possibly a building from which it operates. Creditors might want to seize these assets. It might be prudent to "house" such assets in a separate legal entity, such as a limited liability company (LLC) that protects them from creditors, and have that entity lease the property to the operating company. In such a case, a lease agreement with reasonable terms should exist.

For working persons, disability insurance should be considered when there are insufficient assets to provide for protection in the event of disability. In this regard, Social Security disability benefits are relatively limited.

The Need for a Will, Etc. Property generally passes at death via one of three ways—by will/intestate succession, death beneficiary designation or deed. Things owned outright by a person and not subject to death beneficiary laws or rules, such as a car, pass by will or intestate succession. Retirement plan assets and life insurance benefits pass by death beneficiary designation. A form ordinarily is completed to designate a beneficiary. A default person or group is the beneficiary or beneficiaries if no one is designated. Real estate generally passes by deed. For example, if a husband and wife own their home jointly with the right of survivorship and one spouse dies, the survivor automatically becomes the outright owner.

Regardless of whether taxes are in issue, everyone who is an adult and who owns significant property should have a will. Otherwise, property that would ordinarily transfer in accordance with the terms of a will following death will transfer pursuant to intestate succession (i.e. state intestacy law). The results might not be desirable. For example, Georgia intestacy law provides that a spouse shares equally with the children, provided that the spouse receives at least one-third of the estate. If a child is a minor, separate accounts generally must be maintained to hold a child's share of the assets passing to the child, with those assets payable to the child upon attaining a certain age specified by state law (generally, 18).

Generally, a will can be drafted to prevent an undesirable bequest (e.g. one to a disabled person that destroys his/her eligibility for public aid), and to name the guardian of children in the event of death. It can also provide for assets that would ordinarily be payable to a minor or someone not of a specific age (e.g. 21), to be held in trust until a certain age (e.g. 30) is, or ages (if split into shares, etc.) are, reached.

In some states, particularly those where probating of assets is expensive, a revocable trust that becomes irrevocable upon death, coupled with a "pour over" will, might a better option that simply using a will. The trust will often call for termination and distribution of its assets following death and receipt of any assets received under the pour over will. The pour over will provides that its assets are payable to the trust. A benefit is the will can be very generic. It might simply say that all assets pass to the revocable trust. Because wills are probated, they generally are potentially viewable by the general public through a probate court. In contrast, a trust is generally not viewable by the public. So, using a revocable trust can add privacy and cost savings to an estate plan.

The common problem with revocable trusts is people often do not fund the trust, meaning the assets not owned by the trust must be run through probate (and pass via the pour over will's terms). Furthermore, while a will requires retitling of assets once (following death), a funded revocable trust requires retitling twice—once during life and then again upon distribution of the assets from the trust after death. So, unless privacy, etc. is important, it seems the revocable trust/pour over will option is less desirable than simply using a will (only) in states that have a simple and uncostly probate system (such as Georgia).

Along with a will (or revocable trust and a will), many persons also create a financial power of attorney, authorizing another to make financial decisions for them, perhaps immediately or, alternatively, upon a later possible event such as disability. Issues can arise over whether a power of attorney must be followed by the person to whom it is presented. Often, a bank will demand that its power of attorney be used in order for it to be honored. The lawfulness of such an act will turn on state law, which often is murky in this regard. Georgia changed its law relating to powers of attorney in 2017 and 2018 to generally make it easier to enforce a financial power of attorney.

States have mechanisms for people to choose a health care agent to make decisions for them in the event of incapacity. They are often called a health care power of attorney. Also, in some states, "living wills" can be created, that allow a person to direct an agent how to act with respect to them (and their body) when they are near death or incapacitated and unable to make decisions. Georgia has an "advanced directive," which allows a chosen agent to make both health care decisions while incapacitated and decisions regarding things like disposition of the body after death and guardianship in the event of disability. The generic form can be found on the internet. It costs little or nothing to create these documents. Everyone should have them.

Trusts. A trust can potentially provide asset protection from creditors. Basically, a trust is a legal relationship to property. A person (the grantor) forms a trust by contributing property to the trust, ordinarily in accordance with the terms of a written trust document. The property is held by a trustee, who often is not the grantor, as legal owner for the benefit of one or more beneficiaries. The trustee has a fiduciary duty to act prudently and in the best interests of the beneficiaries. Sometimes, a trust has different beneficiaries, and legal issues can arise therefrom. For example, a trust might provide for the payment of income annually to the one or more beneficiaries, and payment of the trust assets to the remainder beneficiary(ies) when then trust terminates. (Note: The term "generally" is often used below, because state laws are mainly in issue, and those laws vary.)

Generally speaking, a creditor can get from a trust whatever the debtor can get from the trust, but no more. If assets are transferred to a trust when the grantor is solvent, and the transfer does not cause the grantor to become insolvent, then the assets *generally* are protected from the grantor's creditors. Depending on state law, creditors may be able to reach trust assets for the benefit of a beneficiary to the extent the beneficiary has withdrawal rights. (If a non-beneficiary decides upon withdrawals, assets that are not distributed should be safe.) If a beneficiary does not have a right to a distribution, then a creditor generally cannot reach the beneficiary's interest in the trust. However, the IRS generally can take a beneficiary's interest in a trust to satisfy a federal tax deficiency, if that interest can be ascertained.

Some trusts (i.e. grantor trusts) are designed to be deemed nonexistent for tax purposes, so that their earnings and losses flow to the grantor. A revocable trust is a form of grantor trust. They are often used in estate planning in states with heavy probate costs and/or burdens. Upon death, the trust becomes irrevocable. The terms of the revocable trust often call for payment of the trust's assets to the beneficiaries following death. However, revocable trust assets generally can be accessed by a grantor's creditors to the extent the decedent's probate estate is inadequate to pay debts. A possible exception to the rule exists for amounts that could have passed by beneficiary designation.

A spendthrift trust is a trust designed to prevent the beneficiary from wasting assets placed in trust for his or her benefit. It will limit a beneficiary's ability to receive distributions. Georgia law provides that the interest of a beneficiary other than the grantor generally cannot be reached by creditors when the trustee has discretionary distribution powers except to satisfy alimony, child support, taxes or other government claims, tort judgments and a couple other things.

With respect to a spendthrift trust where the grantor is the beneficiary (sometimes called a Domestic Asset Protection Trust), creditors can reach the assets if the trust is revocable. Generally, creditors can also reach the maximum amount of assets that can be taken out by or for the grantor during his or her lifetime. Some states provide greater benefits to grantors. In this regard, states tend to compete for trust business, and the trend is to find more ways to protect grantors. Delaware usually is on the cusp of advancement. It is often uncertain how a state court will react to such a trust created under the laws of another state.

While a fiduciary is potentially liable for failure to act prudently and in the best interest of the beneficiary, generally, absent fault, etc. by the trustee or beneficiary, neither the trustee nor the beneficiary is liable if property owned by the trust results in injury to a person.

Generally speaking, a trust that is not a grantor trust is a separate tax-paying entity. From an income tax perspective, a trust that accumulates income generally is not a good vehicle because a trust reaches the highest federal income tax rate (37 percent) when income reaches $12,751 (for 2019). Generally, a trust is entitled to a deduction for distributions made to beneficiaries. An estate is subject to the same income tax rate system as a trust.

For tax purposes, there are two types of trusts with respect to income accumulation: (a) those that require all of their income to be distributed each year (i.e. a simple trust); and (b) those that do not require all of their income to be distributed each year (i.e. a complex trust). A complex trust could have very flexible terms, such that income might or might not be distributed, perhaps with certain criteria to be analyzed by the trustee pursuant to trust terms to determine whether a distribution should be made. Alternatively, distributions might be left fully to the discretion of the trustee(s).

Example: Sue and Tom, who are married, do not have problems with creditors. They have excess assets that they wish to place in trust to provide for the education and support needs of their children and grandchildren. If a trust is created that provides that a child may withdraw his/her share of income each year, a creditor of the child might be able to access such income amount. (State law would govern.) In contrast, if a trustee was given the power to decide whether and when the separate income shares of the child beneficiaries of a trust should be paid, it is unlikely that any creditor could force the trustee to pay anything to it. So, granting the trustee the power to decide whether a distribution will be made increases asset protection.

Because trusts are subject to a highly progressive income tax regime, it is often desirable to make a trust a grantor trust, so that the grantor, and not the trust, is taxed on the trust's taxable income. A grantor trust is a trust the taxable income and gains of which are not taxed to the trust, but instead are taxed to the grantor or another person if the grantor or other person is treated as an owner.

As noted below, there are several means of making a trust a grantor trust. Sometimes, the grantor desires to make a completed gift for estate and gift tax purposes, but desires for the taxable income of the trust to be taxed to the grantor (so as to reduce income taxes). An "intentionally defective grantor trust" is sometimes used for this purpose. Such a trust provides a complete and irrevocable gift for estate and gift tax purposes (thus taking the property out of the grantor's estate) while causing the grantor to be taxed on the trust's annual net income.

A question that sometimes arises is whether a parent who holds assets as a custodian for the benefit of his child or children can transfer those assets to a separate trust or trusts for the benefit of the (or each) child. The concern here is that a child can do as he/she wishes with the assets upon attaining the age of majority, and the result might not be desirable. The first question that needs to be answered is whether the Uniform Transfers to Minors Act (UMTA) applies and, if so, what are the ramifications? Often with variations, most states have adopted the UTMA. It provides for a transfer of property to minors, with an adult serving as custodian until the child reaches the age of majority in the state. The UTMA only applies in certain cases and the implications of it not applying are often uncertain.

A trust is a grantor trust if the owner has one of the rights described in Internal Revenue Code sections 673-677. These rights generally include the right to reversion (i.e. the right to receive the trust's assets upon termination (section 673)), the right to control beneficial enjoyment of trust assets or income (section 674), the right to administer the trust in significant ways (section 675), the right to revoke the trust (section 676) and the right to receive the trust's income (section 677). A person other than the grantor is treated as the owner under Code section 678 to the extent he or she has the power to transfer the assets or income to himself or herself or if the person can acquire certain power described in Code sections 673-677 in certain circumstances.

If a grantor trust is desired, the question then becomes how to create such a trust. Aside from revocability, the three most common means of making a trust a grantor trust (that are included in Code sections 673-677) probably are the power of the trust to make loans to the grantor without adequate interest or security, the power to add a charitable beneficiary and the power to substitute assets.

Example. Joe wishes to transfer some of his ownership interests in his wholly-owned LLC to a trust for the benefit of his son, but desires for the income or loss to be reported on Joe's income tax return. Joe establishes an irrevocable trust with the right of Joe to substitute assets of equal value, and transfers a membership interest to the trust. Upon funding of the trust, the interest is treated as gifted by Joe, and is no longer deemed owned by Joe for estate tax purposes. (So, the trust is an intentionally defective grantor trust.) Any future income from the trust will be need to be reported by Joe on his income tax return.

Generally speaking, a trustee has a duty to act as a fiduciary for the benefit of the beneficiary of the trust. A power to make a loan for less than adequate interest or without adequate consideration (or both) could run afoul of this duty. Also, the ability to substitute assets must not exist in a fiduciary capacity. Stating in the trust instrument that the trustee could exchange property in non-fiduciary capacity would be risky. Creating a trust with a power to exchange property while not acting as a fiduciary might violate state law.

IRA Protections. As noted in Chapter 8, if a prohibited transaction occurs with respect to an IRA, the IRA is deemed disqualified on the first day of the year of the prohibited transaction. The assets of the IRA are deemed distributed to the IRA owner or beneficiary in a taxable event and the IRA ceases to exist. If the deemed payee is under age 59½, a ten percent (10%) penalty ordinarily also applies.

If there is a concern that a transaction to be undertaken with respect to an IRA could possibly be a prohibited transaction, it would be best to transfer (or roll over) the assets to be involved in the transaction to a separate IRA before undertaking the transaction. IRAs are not aggregated when a prohibited transaction analysis is undertaken, meaning a disqualification of an IRA due to a prohibited transaction will have no bearing on any other IRAs.

Example: Dave has an IRA with $800,000 in assets. He wishes to use $150,000 of his IRA assets to buy a house to rent to a potential tenant. Dave has been advised that there might be some prohibited transaction concerns with respect to the house purchase and ownership. He can roll over $150,000 of the $800,000 of benefits to a new IRA and undertake the investment in the new IRA, thus preventing any risk with respect to the remaining $650,000 of IRA assets.

IRA benefits are not assignable. So, while living, except in the case of divorce, IRA assets cannot be transferred to another person's IRA. Sometimes, a large share of a couple's wealth is held in the form of tax-qualified plan and/or IRA benefits of one spouse. If the marriage is solid and is a first marriage, such a scenario ordinarily is not problematic. Benefits in tax-qualified plans can be kept there or transferred to an IRA. Most plans permit lump-sum distributions. In the solid first marriage situation, the spouse with the benefits can name the other spouse as death beneficiary. Then, when the IRA owner dies, the other spouse can roll the assets over to his or her IRA. (If the assets are in an IRA, the spouse can instead have the IRA treated as his or her own IRA.) The surviving spouse can take benefits as needed for living. If there are children, the surviving spouse would ordinarily name them as death beneficiaries. The children could receive distributions of the residual assets over their life expectancies or earlier.

If the facts of the preceding paragraph differ in that the marriage is a second marriage with children from the first marriage, things can get dicey. If the accounts belong to the husband and he has children from his first marriage, he will likely wish to provide that at least some of the benefits will be paid to his children. A spouse ordinarily is the death beneficiary of tax-qualified plan assets absent a written waiver by the spouse. However, IRAs have no such requirement. If the husband wishes to provide for his spouse but also provide for his children after he dies, there are at least two options. First, he could split the death beneficiaries of the plan(s)/account(s) between the spouse and the children. If the assets are held in one account, he should be able to designate different beneficiaries and percentages for the account. (Spousal consent will be necessary for tax-qualified plan assets.) If the assets are in different places (e.g. some in an IRA and some in a tax-qualified plan), some calculations would need to be performed to split as desired. Second, he could establish an IRA trust to take care of the spouse while she is living, with the remainder assets passing to the children following her death.

An IRA trust could be established and named as death beneficiary, pursuant to the trust's terms. The minimum required distribution ("MRD") rules of Internal Revenue Code section 401(a)(9) would need to be met, with the trust as payee. These rules require that certain MRDs be taken beginning in the year following the year in which the IRA owner attains age 70½. Also, certain regulatory requirements would need to be met by the trust. However, once received by the trust, depending on trust terms, the assets could either be immediately distributed or retained by the trust. (Keep in mind the undesirable income tax rules applicable to income retained by trusts that are not grantor trusts.) The trustee of an IRA trust could be permitted to withdraw more than MRDs, such as distributions necessary to maintain the living standard of a surviving spouse.

The income tax regulations under Code section 401(a)(9) need to be thoroughly analyzed when creating such a trust. Generally, the life expectancy of the oldest beneficiary must be used to compute MRDs. Thus, "subtrusts" are sometimes created, so that each beneficiary's life expectancy can be used for his/her interest. Each subtrust should be named as a separate beneficiary. Alternatively, to be safer, separate trusts could be created for one or more IRAs. A subtrust could possibly be created for the spouse and each child, with the spouse's remaining benefit payable to the child(ren) following her death.

An IRA trust could provide protection from creditors of a beneficiary. For example, if the trust provided that only MRDs would be distributed, a creditor could only potentially garnish the MRD. The trust might be drafted to permit MRDs to be accumulated by the trustee, if the trustee decided that accumulation was in the best interest of the beneficiary.

Example: Sam and Debbie have been married for many years. They are about to retire, and they plan on living off their IRA savings and Social Security for many years following retirement. They have two children: Jack and Jill. Jack was always a problem child, and his problems have carried over into adulthood. He has problems with creditors and substance abuse. Jill is self-sufficient and responsible. A safety technique might be to make Jill the death beneficiary of half of all IRA assets remaining upon the death of the survivor of Sam and Debbie (with the survivor of Sam and Debbie first being paid via roll over or election the remaining benefits of the deceased one of them), while leaving the other half to a trust for the benefit of Jack that meets the MRD rules and grants the trustee discretion as to when Jack will be entitled to distributions.

Disabled Persons. Means of protecting assets relating to disabled persons, and to prevent loss of their public benefits, are covered in Chapter 10. It is important to note that when a document is created (e.g. a will), a person might not be disabled, but the person could become disabled in the future. As discussed in Chapter 10, an inheritance by a disabled person could disqualify them from public disability benefits (due to excessive wealth).

Tax Deficiencies. If a tax deficiency exists, there are a number of asset protection strategies to consider. The IRS is the most powerful creditor in the U.S., as it does not need to take a taxpayer to court to collect on a tax deficiency. Rather, the liability generally is set by the tax return and an insufficient tax payment. The IRS only needs to send out notices of its intent to collect, and then wait a period of time (generally, 30 days) before taking a taxpayer's assets.

Sometimes, the IRS need not give advance notice of its intent to levy on (i.e. take) assets.

If a tax deficiency exists, and the taxpayer believes the assessment is incorrect or excessive, the taxpayer should act as quickly as reasonably possible to contest the deficiency. The IRS can collect interest and penalties for late payment. In recent years, the interest rates have been very reasonable (3 to 6 percent per year), but the penalties can be substantial. If a deficiency exists, and there is no dispute as to it, the simplest thing to do if the deficiency is relatively small is to pay it.

If a large deficiency exists that is not disputed, and payment in full is not practical, then there are three common options. First, the taxpayer can enter into an installment payment agreement to pay all or part of the deficiency plus interest over a period of years. Often, the IRS will allow the period to be six years. While the IRS likes an installment agreement to cover all of the deficiency, they might agree to it covering less. Second, the taxpayer can file an offer-in-compromise, attempting to reduce the tax debt to an amount it can pay. The IRS requires an individual to complete Form 433-A to determine the amount that should be offered. The IRS requires the taxpayer to report on Form 433-A all of his or her assets, some liabilities such as a home mortgage and anticipated cash flow from income and expenses. The IRS then demands payment based on the combination of net worth and anticipated cash flow. Only certain expenses are permissible in the cash flow analysis. For some assets, a discount (e.g. 20 percent) applies to account for illiquidity and potential taxes. Third, the taxpayer can file bankruptcy. However, generally, bankruptcy will discharge only income taxes with respect to which the due date of the return was more than three years prior to the filing of bankruptcy and the return was filed more than two years prior to the bankruptcy filing.

Like most creditors, the IRS first looks for low-hanging fruit. Generally, it will first garnish wages and levy on bank accounts to take any cash in such accounts. Ordinarily, the IRS does not pursue a taxpayer's residence to recover the tax debt, as it requires going to court and having a federal judge approve of the taking. Retirement funds are also not a desired source, as taking them reduces the taxpayer's ability to eventually retire. The IRS's general policy is to pursue retirement assets only if the taxpayer has been contributing to a retirement account instead of paying the IRS, or has acted unreasonably in the collections process. Some lawful things can be done for legitimate business reasons to make attempting to access the taxpayer's assets unappealing to the IRS.

Taxpayers often get consumed with the debt they owe the IRS, while forgetting about related state tax liabilities. While the states generally are slower than the IRS to pursue a tax debtor, they are often more aggressive (and sometimes ruthless) in their collection efforts. Some states charge a very high interest rate with respect to tax deficiencies. Until recently, Georgia was such a state.

Marriage Risks. Divorce can take away substantial wealth. State law determines how assets owned by married persons are split in the event of divorce. Certain persons may wish to enter into a pre-marital (prenuptial) agreement to limit potential wealth loss in the event of divorce.

State laws will specify whether a prenuptial agreement is lawful, and (if so) the conditions for such an agreement to be enforceable. State laws may require the prospective spouses to disclose their net worth in advance of entering into the agreement. Also, agreement terms must not be unconscionable.

Other Considerations. Diversification reduces risk. To the extent feasible, assets owned should be diversified among different investment types, including real estate and stocks. In an era of regular identity theft, action should be taken to protect identification numbers and similar things, including (of course) one's Social Security number. Companies exist that provide protection services. Means of supplying account access, etc. to loved ones following death or disability should be handled, including through a power of attorney. Emails access should also be considered.

To the extent assets are retained in a bank account, it is important to note how Federal Deposit Insurance Corporation (FDIC) protection works. The FDIC insures against bank failure in the amount of $250,000 per depositor at the insured bank, for each account ownership category. The account ownership categories generally used by individuals are single accounts, certain retirement accounts, joint accounts, revocable trust accounts, irrevocable trust accounts, employee benefit plan accounts and business entity accounts. Each of these accounts generally includes checking, savings, CD and money market accounts within them. So, for example, a person owning $90,000 apiece (total of $270,000) in personal (i.e. single) checking, savings and money market accounts at one bank would receive insurance of $250,000 for the combination of these accounts. So, $20,000 would go uninsured. Opening an account at another bank for $20,000 or more of the funds would protect all of the funds.

Chapter 4

Legal Entity Options for Doing Business

The most significant issues in choosing a type of legal entity in which to do business relate to liability exposure and taxes. Virtually all desire to minimize both. The types of business entity that can be used turn on whether there will be one or two or more owners of the business.

With respect to a business to be owned by one person, the options are sole proprietorship (i.e. do nothing), C corporation, S corporation and limited liability company (LLC). A sole proprietor simply reports the business income or loss on his or her personal income tax return. No liability protection whatsoever exists for the sole proprietor. As explained below, to be anything other than a sole proprietorship, a filing must be made and a fee must be paid to a state.

Corporations are determined by state non-tax law and, for state law purposes, there is no such thing as an S corporation or a C corporation. Rather, there are for-profit and nonprofit corporations. (States generally recognize federal C and S corporation status when applying their tax laws.) The shareholders of for-profit corporations ordinarily are not liable for the debts of the corporation. Ordinarily, nonprofit corporations do not have shareholders.

The LLC is a relatively new phenomenon. In the 1980s, Wyoming and Florida were the first states to provide for LLCs. Prior to LLCs, many businesses were structured as limited partnerships. The benefit of a partnership (including a limited partnership) is the partnership "flow through" tax rules apply, so that the business never pays income tax. Rather, the income and losses of the business are passed through to the owners for inclusion on their income tax returns.

The drawback of a limited partnership was (and is) that at least one partner must be a general partner and a general partner is potentially liable for all of the debts of the business (i.e. if the business does not pay them). In contrast, an LLC ordinarily receives the tax benefits of a partnership while providing all owners (i.e. members) with liability protection. The amount potentially at risk to members of an LLC for liabilities of an LLC ordinarily is only the capital contributed.

With respect to a business owned by two or more persons, business form options include a general partnership, a limited partnership, an S corporation, a C corporation and an LLC. Many states have variations on limited partnerships and LLCs, particularly for professionals. For example, a state might have a law that provides for a special form of LLC or limited partnership (e.g. a limited liability partnership—LLP) that provides that an owner is not liable for the liabilities of the business that do not relate to professional practice, but is subject to liabilities relating to professional practice.

Most states have laws that prohibit professionals from insulating themselves from liability for malpractice. Thus, even if an entity ordinarily would protect a member from liability for actions of the entity (whether the entity is a corporation, LLC or limited partnership), the professional owners of the business would remain potentially liable for acts of malpractice. Whether an individual who is an owner of an entity can potentially be liable for malpractice actions of a fellow owner of the entity will depend on state law. Thus, most professionals purchase malpractice insurance.

A general partnership is taxed in the same manner as a limited partnership. However, all owners are potentially liable for the debts of the business. Accordingly, these entities are rarely used. A business owned by two or more persons or entities that does not file with a state of residence and pay a fee to be something other than a general partnership ordinarily will be treated as a general partnership.

An S corporation typically is a state law for-profit corporation or LLC that has elected to be taxed under Subchapter S of the Internal Revenue Code. Limits exist on S eligibility. In general, an S corporation cannot have more than one-hundred (100) owners (i.e. shareholders or members) and all of the owners must be U.S. residents. Exceptions exist.

S corporation shareholders generally must be individuals. However, four types of trusts can be S shareholders. A shareholders' agreement with respect to an S corporation may provide that if a shareholder permits his shares to be held by a trust, the shareholder will cause the trustee of the trust to take all necessary and appropriate action to maintain the trust as a permissible shareholder of an S corporation. (The four types of trusts that can be an S company shareholder are a grantor trust, a Qualified Subchapter S Trust ("QSST"), an electing small business trust and a voting trust. Each type of trust could be created to provide for distribution of all of the income of the trust currently. However, only a QSST is required to distribute its income currently. There are pros and cons to each type.)

An S corporation is generally taxed in a similar manner to a partnership (such that tax ordinarily is not payable by the corporation), except the corporation sometimes can be subject to tax and the owners do not have any flexibility to allocate profits or losses in a manner that varies from their equity share of the business. For example, a 25 percent shareholder would need to "pick up" (i.e. report) 25 percent of the profits or losses of the S corporation on his or her income tax return, whereas a partnership (or an LLC taxable as a partnership) could possibly vary allocations of profits and losses to owners in different ways in different years. There are some limits on this flexibility.

A C corporation ordinarily is a state law for-profit corporation that is not an S corporation. It is subject to taxation under Subchapter C of the Internal Revenue Code. As amended by the Tax Cuts and Jobs Act (TCJA), Subchapter C provides for a flat 21 percent income tax applicable to taxable income of the corporation. Distributions of profits to C corporation shareholders are then subject to tax *again*, although the capital gains tax rate applies to such dividend distributions if the corporation is a domestic corporation (i.e. incorporated under the laws of a U.S. state) or a certain type of foreign corporation. Certain other taxes can apply to C corporations, including a tax on a failure to distribute a sufficient amount of accumulated earnings.

Example: Donna owns 25 percent of the shares of stock of an S corporation. The S corporation earned $100,000 in 2019. Donna must report $25,000 of the S corporation's profits on her 2019 individual income tax return, regardless of whether any money or property was distributed to her. If the corporation was instead a C corporation, the corporation would have paid federal (and likely state) income tax on its $100,000 profit. For 2019, the federal income tax would have been $21,000. Any distribution of the remaining profit of $79,000 (i.e. $100,000 - $21,000) would potentially be subject to capital gains tax to Donna.

If a business is expected to produce losses (perhaps because it is a "startup" company), the owners will often want the losses to "flow through" to them, so that their shares can be reported on their income tax returns. As noted in Chapter 5, the passive loss rules can potentially limit the ability of a business owner to take losses. To the extent those rules don't present a problem, the entity type may have an impact on the ability to pass-through losses. Both an LLC and an S corporation will provide for pass-through of losses. However, as explained in more detail in Chapter 5, the accumulated loss share of a shareholder of an S corporation generally can be taken only to the extent of the amount of equity in the company plus the amount loaned to the company by the shareholder. In contrast, an LLC member or a partner in a partnership generally can deduct accumulated losses to the extent of his equity plus his share of the entity's debts. The share of debt owed by a member or partner depends on various factors.

In the 1990s, the IRS adopted the "check the box" regulations. Under these rules, certain persons and entities can elect to be taxed in a certain manner, and certain default rules apply. A form is ordinarily used to elect a taxation manner other than the default method of taxation. A sole proprietorship can elect to be treated as C corporation or an S corporation, with the default being sole proprietor treatment. The same rules apply to an LLC owned by one person. Most businesses other than corporations owned by two or more persons can elect to be taxed as a partnership, C corporation or S corporation. The default for an LLC is taxation as a partnership. A state law corporation, however, will be treated as a C corporation unless its shareholders elect to be taxed as an S corporation. At least prior to 2018, making an S election generally was beneficial.

For persons who work for the business, the income that flows to them for inclusion on their income tax returns will ordinarily be subject to self-employment (SECA) tax as well as income tax. However, as noted in the chart below, exceptions exist.

Given the choice, what's the best form of entity?

Prior to 2018, in order to potentially avoid double taxation, being something other than a C corporation was almost always desirable. However, TCJA reduced taxes applicable to C corporations by replacing a graduated rate structure with a highest rate of 35 percent with a flat 21 percent rate. As discussed in Chapter 5, under Code §1202, the gain on sale of the stock of certain C corporations is completely tax-free. So, after 2017, being a C corporation can potentially be more appealing.

As thoroughly explained in Chapter 5, TCJA created a deduction for sole proprietors and individual owners of S corporations, partnerships and LLCs. The deduction generally is 20 percent of the net taxable income of a trade or business. Also, TCJA reduced the maximum individual income tax rate to 37 percent, causing the maximum net federal rate applicable to pass-through entities (and a sole proprietorship) to be 29.6 percent (i.e. .37 x .80) if the full 20 percent deduction applies. However, the deduction can be less than 20 percent, and it does not apply to the income of most very high-earning professionals.

Generally, for an individual sole owner, a single member LLC that does not elect to be taxed as something other than a sole proprietorship is the best form of entity. This is so because the owner has liability protection from the debts of the business, the LLC is not subject to tax, and the owner can simply report the profit or loss of the business on Schedule C of his or her income tax return.

Also, it generally costs little to form and maintain an LLC. However, exceptions exist, such as the example discussed at the end of Chapter 7 (wherein S corporation treatment is preferable), relating to federal financial aid for college.

Example: Bill, who is a CPA, has an accounting practice. He has not done anything in terms of entity status with his state of residence. Accordingly, the practice is a sole proprietorship. For $100, Bill can form a state law LLC for his practice. As the sole member, the entity would be disregarded for income tax purposes, meaning he will continue to report the earnings on Schedules C and SE of his Form 1040, income tax return. However, in the event of most liability matters (but likely excluding malpractice), he will be protected from potential exposure for the practice's liabilities.

Generally speaking, for a business owned by more than one person, an LLC that does not elect to be taxed as something other than a partnership is the best form of entity. This is so because the owners have liability protection from the debts of the business, the LLC is not subject to tax, and the owners can simply report their shares of the profit or loss of the business on their income tax returns. Also, if the business borrows money and has losses, the ability of LLC members to take the losses ordinarily is increased by their shares of the debts. However, an S corporation sometimes is a better choice of entity. This may be so when there will be little debt or most or all of the debt is owed to the shareholders and one or more of the owners works only part-time for the businesses, thus providing for the possibility of paying reasonable salaries and causing the remainder of the businesses profits to flow through to the owners as profits that are not subject to the SECA tax. In contrast, an LLC member ordinary would need to include in SECA income his share of the LLC's profits. Certain retirement plans might be better suited for an S corporation that an LLC. With TCJA, a C corporation could be best under certain circumstances, including a situation where profits are very high (e.g. over $600,000+ per owner) and are not distributed for many years.

Example: Joe is a married one-third owner of an LLC that made an S election. He and his spouse file a joint tax return. After paying each shareholder $100,000 of reasonable compensation each year, the business averages $300,000 of profit. The average profit per owner is $100,000. Using the 20 percent deduction of TCJA (see Chapter 5 note), each owner would report $80,000 of income with respect to the business. Assuming each owner took only the standard deduction, federal tax for 2019 would be $25,949. In contrast, if the business elected to be a C corporation, the company would pay federal tax of $63,000 ($21,000 per owner). Also, distributions of remaining profits would be qualified dividends that would likely be taxed at a 0 or 15 percent rate. Assuming no state tax on net income, the total distributable would be $237,000. At 15 percent, each member's share of $79,000 would bear capital gains tax of $11,850, bringing each owner's tax total to $32,850 (i.e. 21,000 + 11,850). If distributions were not immediately made, but instead were deferred for many years, then C status could be better. State tax considerations could also be significant. (Note: This example assumes no other income or deductions.)

Some people make an S election for a sole proprietorship, pay themselves a salary and receive the balance of the net income of the business as a profit distribution (or deemed distribution). This is done to minimize FICA/SECA tax. For example, if profit before a salary for the owner is $200,000 in 2019, paying a $50,000 salary and receiving $150,000 of profit would reduce FICA/SECA tax for 2019 by $14,629.60. The calculations are as follows: (((132,900 − 50,000) x .124) + ((200,000 - 50,000) x .029))). (As noted in Chapter 5: The Social Security Wage Base (SSWB) for 2019 is $132,900. The Social Security tax rate and Medicare tax rate applicable to self-employed persons are, respectively, 12.4 percent and 2.9 percent. For employees' wages, the employer pays half of this tax and the employees pay half. The Social Security tax does not apply to earned income above the SSWB but the Medicare rate applies to all earned income. Profits aren't earned income.) This strategy legitimately works if some profit can be attributed to someone or something other than the owner's efforts and the salary amount is reasonable.

Example: Ron is the sole owner of a business that employs several employees. The business is an LLC that has not made any tax election (so it is a disregarded entity for federal tax purposes—i.e. like a sole proprietorship). Ron works for the business on a part-time basis, as he has a regular full-time job. The business has become very successful. The profit for 2019 was $200,000. If the business is an LLC, Ron must report $200,000 of profit for both income tax and SECA tax purposes. The SECA tax would be $22,279.60. Ron does some research and determines that a reasonable salary for what he does would be $100,000. If Ron had (instead of keeping LLC tax status) made an S election for the business and paid himself a $100,000 salary, there would be no change in his income tax, but his SECA/FICA tax would have decreased by $6,979.60 to $15,300. If Ron makes $32,900 or more at his regular full-time job, his future Social Security benefits would not be diminished because his total salary would not be below the 2019 Social Security Wage Base of $132,900. Note: As explained in Chapter 5, computation of the SECA tax is slightly more complicated and the tax base is slightly less than that noted in this example and above because one-half of the tentative tax is deductible. This example and the above text provide a rough differential.

Some businesses that could be something other than a C corporation are C corporations. These businesses often "zero out" their earnings to avoid double taxation and to take advantage of certain cafeteria plan benefits that are available to C corporations. (A cafeteria plan is one that permits employees to choose between cash and one or more nontaxable benefits, such as health care. If cash is elected by an employee, the cash is included in income. If a nontaxable benefit is elected, the benefit is not included in income.) However, if the profits are attributable to work other than that of the owners, there is a risk the IRS will, upon audit (if it audits), reallocate some of the compensation of the owners to profit, thus resulting in entity level (and potentially double) taxation.

As noted, corporations and LLCs generally provide protection from liability for the owners of the company with respect to the company's debts. If the company has a legal dispute, sometimes the person or entity opposing the company in the litigation will attempt to "pierce the corporate veil." If company's corporate veil is pierced, the owners of the business are liable for the debts of the company. The ability to pierce the veil varies by state law.

Some things can be done by both a corporation and an LLC to minimize the risk of piercing of the corporate veil. They include:

(a)   Letterheads, billing heads, etc. should reflect the full name of the company;

(b)   Business cards should use the company name;

(c)   The company's bank checking account should use the company name;

(d)   Telephone listing and listing in all directories should reflect the company name;

(e)   All leases, contracts and other arrangements should be in the name of the company;

(f)   The name on the company's place of business should reflect the company name;

(g)   Insurance should be carefully reviewed to determine if the company business is properly insured and that the company and the owners individually are properly protected; if real property is transferred to the company, generally, the company should be named as an additional insured on any insurance policies covering the real property;

(h)   No personal expenditures or private transactions should be made by the company; all loans and other transactions between the company and the shareholders or members should be carefully documented; accurate accounting records are a must; and

(i) Adequate capitalization should be maintained; the necessary amount will depend on the nature of the business and the amount of insurance purchased; in many cases, a small amount (e.g. $500) is all that is necessary.

With respect to both corporations and LLCs with more than one owner, a creditor of an owner cannot force a liquidation of the entity when the owner owes a debt to the creditor. Generally, the creditor is limited to relief in the form of a "charging order," whereby the creditor becomes entitled to whatever distributions, etc. the debtor would ordinarily be entitled to receive from the business. Both a corporation and an LLC can have protections in place to prevent a creditor from becoming an owner (such as requiring sale or liquidation of an interest in the event of collection action by a creditor of an owner against the business). The ordinary protection for a corporation will be found in a shareholders' agreement. The ordinary protection for an LLC will be found in the operating agreement. For a private corporation, a shareholders' agreement should virtually always exist, to cover things such a death, disability or insolvency of a shareholder.

Things like death and disability of an owner should be taken into account in the operating agreement of an LLC or the bylaws or shareholders' agreement with respect to a corporation. An owner might be shocked to find that his or her business partner is his or her former's partner's spouse following the death of the former partner. Such a document could also deal with matters like offers made to one, but less than all, of the owners. For example, in a two persons company, the ability to sell might be made contingent on the buyer purchasing both owners' interests on the same terms.

Whenever a business (corporation, LLC or partnership) will have multiple owners, there may need to be tie-breaker considerations. For example, often, two individuals wish to form an LLC or a corporation, with the two owners having equal control. What happens if they fail to agree upon something (as inevitably will very likely happen)? Some businesses "muddle through" and the owners resolve their differences and reach a consensus. But, what if that doesn't happen? In such a situation, there needs to be a tie-breaker for the unresolved issues. For an LLC, the operating agreement would ordinarily supply the mechanism. For a corporation, the mechanism might be in the bylaws or a shareholders agreement. Various means of resolving a tie vote situation exist, although none are great. If two members or shareholders exist, they might agree to appoint a mutually accepted person to break the tie, or use a coin toss if they cannot agree on a decider.

The chart below lists considerations with respect to the various forms of entities, with Georgia law as the state system:

LEGAL (GEORGIA) AND TAX COMPARISON OF SOLE PROPRIETORSHIP, PARTNERSHIP/LLC, S CORPORATION, AND C CORPORATION

FACTOR:	SOLE PRO-PRIETORSHIP	PARTNERSHIP/LLC[1,2]	S CORPORATION	C CORPORATION
A. Initial Formation Of Entity	N/A; no cost	Very simple and virtually always tax-free; costs usually low	Ordinarily, not complex. Almost always tax-free at the corporate level; exception potentially exists if liabilities exceed basis of assets transferred; cost usually low	Ordinarily, not complex. Almost always tax-free; exception potentially exists if liabilities exceed basis of assets transferred; costs usually low
B. Legal Liability	Unlimited liability; (Note: A single member LLC can be formed to provide	LLC: Liability limited to capital investment; General Partnership: All partners potentially liable for entity's debts and partners'	Liability limited to capital investment; no individual shareholder liability	Liability limited to capital investment; no individual shareholder liability

---

[1] A single member LLC that is owned by an individual results in taxation of the individual in the same manner as a sole proprietorship. Thus, the LLC is a disregarded entity for income tax purposes. Similarly, a single member LLC that is owned by an entity is disregarded for tax purposes.
[2] A multiple member LLC is ordinarily taxed as a partnership (and this chart so assumes), although it can elect to be taxed as a C corporation or perhaps as an S corporation.

FACTOR:	SOLE PRO-PRIETORSHIP	PARTNERSHIP/LLC[1,2]	S CORPORATION	C CORPORATION
	limited liability.)	actions; Limited Partnership: Only general partner(s) potentially liable for the entity's debts		
C. Limits on Ownership	N/A	No limits	• no more than 100 shareholders (family members treated as one person) • generally, only individuals can be shareholders • no nonresident alien shareholders • can have only one class of stock (but can have voting and nonvoting stock)	No limits
D. Confidentiality of Owners, Officers, Managers	Very difficult to hide identity of owner	GA: Identity of owners/managers of LLC can be kept confidential; partnerships - identity of general partner only is required	GA: Annual registration with Secretary of State reports officers; shareholders not disclosed	GA: Annual registration with Secretary of State reports officers; shareholders not disclosed
E. Annual Income Taxation	Owner picks up all income, gain, expense, loss and credit; up to 20% of profit deduction	Tax never paid; all income, gain, expense, loss and credits flow through to partners; Flexibility to	S corporations ordinarily don't pay tax;[3] Earnings and losses of S corporations flow through to shareholders pro	C corporations pay tax on taxable income; in <u>Pediatric Surgical Associates P.C. v. Comm'r</u>, T.C.

---

[3] Under §1374 of the Internal Revenue Code, a 21% tax applies to appreciated and certain other assets sold or converted to cash or distributed during the 5-year period beginning on the date of the S election by a corporation that has been a C corporation. Also, under §1375, if an S corporation has accumulated earnings and profits from a period when it was a C corporation, and the corporation's passive investment income exceeds 25% of its gross receipts, then a tax (at the highest corporate tax rate) applies to the excess passive investment income.

FACTOR:	SOLE PRO-PRIETORSHIP	PARTNERSHIP/LLC[1,2]	S CORPORATION	C CORPORATION
	potentially applicable	allocate income/loss generally exists; Partners must include income, gains, expenses, losses and credits on their returns; up to 20% of profit deduction potentially applicable	rata based on shares held; (Distributions to S share-holders must be pro rata based on shares held); up to 20% of profit deduction potentially applicable	Memo 2001-81, IRS converted part of physicians' salaries to corporate profit; Earnings/losses of a C corporation do not pass through to shareholders
F. Annual Earnings & Basis Adjust-ments for Annual Earnings	N/A	Annual earnings taxed to owners, but adjusted basis of partnership interests of partners increased by earnings, alleviating potential for double tax (but distributions and losses reduce adjusted basis)	Annual earnings taxed to owners, but adjusted basis of equity interests of shareholders increased by earnings, alleviating potential for double tax (but distributions and losses reduce adjusted basis)	No basis increase for annual earnings
G. Distributions	No consequences	Distributions need not be pro rata; partnership distributions taxable to partner only if cash and/or readily tradable securities distributed exceed partnership interest adjusted basis; generally, no gain or loss recognized on property distributions and property usually takes a carryover basis in the hands of the partner	Must be pro rata based on stock held; a distribution cannot be made if it will cause the company to be insolvent; unlike partnerships, gain recognized on distribution of appreciated assets, but losses not recognized on distributions of depreciated assets; otherwise, tax-free to extent of undistributed earnings included	Must be pro rata based on stock held; unlike an S corporation, a second class of stock (e.g., preferred stock) can exist. A distribution cannot be made if it will cause the company to be insolvent; gain recognized on distributions of appreciated

FACTOR:	SOLE PRO- PRIETORSHIP	PARTNERSHIP/LLC[1,2]	S CORPORATION	C CORPORATION
			in stock's adjusted basis plus capital contributions[4]	assets, but losses not recognized on distributions of depreciated assets; distributions taxable as dividends to extent of current and accumulated earnings and profits ("E&P")
H. Tax Impact of Debt	No impact	Partners generally share in debts of partnership for purposes of partners' adjusted basis in the partnership interests, including the ability to take losses passed through; nonrecourse liabilities generally shared by all partners; recourse liabilities shared by partners potentially liable	Shareholder receives adjusted basis for amounts loaned to S corporation by the shareholder for loss deductibility purposes only (deductions can be taken to extent of capital contributions, undistributed profits and loans by the shareholder)	No impact
I. FICA	All income subject to FICA tax, except income from an investment	All income of a general partnership except investment income is subject to FICA tax; a limited partners' share of profits is ordinarily not subject to FICA tax; for LLCs, under	Compensation only subject to FICA tax; profits from corporation that flow through are not subject to FICA tax Compensation	C corporations – only compensation subject to FICA tax, but because all taxable income of C corporation

---

[4] An exception exists for S corporations that previously were C corporations and that have accumulated earnings and profits (E&P). In such a case, distributions are tax-free to the extent of previously taxed earnings (i.e. the accumulated adjustments account), then are taxable to the extent of accumulated E&P and are then tax-free to the extent of capital contributions (with gain resulting to the extent of any excess above the capital contributions) .

FACTOR:	SOLE PRO-PRIETORSHIP	PARTNERSHIP/LLC[1,2]	S CORPORATION	C CORPORATION
		proposed regulations (not law), generally taxable, except the share of a non-manager member who does not perform more than 500 hours of service for the LLC for the year is generally exempt, unless the LLC is a professional service LLC and the individual provides professional services; see CCA 201436049	must be reasonable; low compensation means low tax-qualified plan potential benefits	subject to income tax, C corporations often attempt to pay out all profits to shareholders as compensation, making them roughly equal to partnerships from a FICA tax perspective); see prior discussion of Pediatric Surgical Associates case
J. Employee Benefits	Although not certain under the law, appears likely that a self-employed person could have any benefits that are available to a partner; health insurance premiums deductible	Cafeteria plan benefits not available to partners; owners can maintain health insurance and deduct all premiums (after deduction by entity and income inclusion by partner/member); nonqualified plans ordinarily not an attractive option because of annual pass-through of earnings	Cafeteria plan benefits not available to greater than 2% shareholders; owners can maintain health insurance and deduct all premiums (after deduction by entity and income inclusion by shareholders); nonqualified plans ordinarily not an attractive option because of annual pass-through of earnings	Full array of benefits generally available, including nonqualified plans
K. Dissolution	N/A	Debts must be paid before owners can be paid any return on investment; taxable only if cash and value of marketable securities distributed exceeds	Debts must be paid before owners can be paid any return on investment; gain recognized on appreciated assets distributed, but loss not recognized on depreciated	Debts must be paid before owners can be paid any return on investment; gain recognized on appreciated assets

49

FACTOR:	SOLE PRO-PRIETORSHIP	PARTNERSHIP/LLC[1],[2]	S CORPORATION	C CORPORATION
		partner's adjusted basis; otherwise, assets distributed take basis of partnership interest, after reduction for any cash and marketable equity securities received in the dissolution; liquidating distributions must be made in accordance with capital account balances	assets; basis of stock increased by gain recognized, thus prohibiting double taxation; capital gain or loss based on difference between amount distributed (FMV) and the adjusted basis of the stock	distributed, but loss not recognized on depreciated assets; no basis adjustment in stock for gains; capital gain or loss based on difference between amount distributed (FMV) and adjusted basis of the stock
L. Sale of Interests or Assets	Gain recognized; nature (capital gain or ordinary income) depends on type of assets sold	Gain recognized on sale of interest, with composition (capital gain v. ordinary income) dependent upon breakdown of assets held by entity; sale of assets produces gain, the nature of which (capital gain/ordinary income) will depend on the nature of the assets sold	Capital gain recognized on sale of the stock; sale of assets by company produces gain, the nature of which (capital gain or ordinary income) will depend on the type of assets sold; gain pass-through would increase the basis of the shareholder's stock	Capital gain generally recognized on the sale of the stock (exception can exist under §1202); sale of assets by company produces gain, the nature of which (capital gain or ordinary income) will depend on the type of assets sold (unlike S corporation, no basis step-up in shares of shareholders for gain recognized

Chapter 5

The Federal Tax System & Individual Planning

In order to be able to effectively plan from a financial perspective, it is necessary to have a basic understanding of the U.S tax system. A basic summary of the federal tax system applicable to individuals, including changes made by Tax Cuts and Jobs Act of 2017 ("TCJA"), immediately follows. Thereafter, tax planning ideas are supplied.

Overview of the Federal Tax System

For the federal government's fiscal year that began on October 1, 2018, estimated revenue is $3.5 trillion. Roughly 92 percent of that federal revenue will be produced by the income tax and Social Security and Medicare taxes. Fifty-seven percent (57%) will be income tax, of which the corporate income tax will be 7 percent and the individual income tax will be 50 percent, and 35 percent will be Social Security and Medicare taxes. The remaining eight percent of revenue will be comprised of excise taxes, miscellaneous fees and other sources and the estate and gift tax. The 2019 estate and gift tax exemption is $11.4 million, meaning the tax applies only if a person passes or gives that much wealth during life or following death. Less than 0.1 percent of the U.S. population is subject to the tax.

The income tax applies, in different forms, to individuals, certain corporations, trusts and estates. While the income tax was originally enacted to be paid by only a small percent of the population (i.e. the very wealthy), the system was greatly expanded in terms of tax rates and persons subject to the tax during World War II to finance the war effort. After World War II ended, the tax remained largely intact, and the revenue it produced was used to finance federal war debt reduction, the federal highway system and the Cold War.

The current system is very complex. Taxable income, which is the excess of income over deductible expenses, is subject to tax. Calculating income requires an analysis of whether a thing is income and, if so, when it is income, what type of income it is, and the amount. Certain receipts (e.g. a gift or bequest) are not income. Other amounts, such as the proceeds of the sale of shares of common stock, produce capital gain income that is potentially subject to a lower tax rate than the rate applicable to "ordinary income" such as wages.

General Mechanics. Income tax filing status depends on marriage status and whether dependents exist. Unmarried persons file as single, unless they have dependents that permit them to file as head of household (thus reducing tax). Married persons can file their annual income tax return either jointly or separately. Generally, it is best for them to file jointly if one spouse has substantially more income than the other spouse. Tax software can be purchased to run a couple's return both ways. Some software provides for tax planning for the current year.

There are different methods of accounting for income tax purposes. Virtually all individuals, small businesses and some mid-sized businesses use the cash method of accounting, where income is recognized when cash or property is received (or constructively received) and expenses are recognized when payments are made. Large and some mid-sized companies use the accrual method of accounting, wherein income is recognized when earned and expenses are recorded when liabilities are incurred to pay for goods or services received. Regardless of the method used, generally, assets having a useful life of more than a year must be "capitalized" and "written off" (i.e. depreciated or amortized) over their statutorily-specified useful life.

Generally, personal service corporations, partnerships without C corporation partners, S corporations and other pass-through entities are allowed to use the cash method of accounting, as long as it clearly reflects income. Also, a business with average annual gross receipts not in excess of $25 million for three consecutive years can use the cash method. Subject to the $25 million/3-year average exception, companies possessing inventory generally must use the accrual method. Hybrids exist, such as use of the cash method while capitalizing certain expenses and recording inventory. Under TCJA, an accrual method taxpayer must recognize income no later than the year it is recognized for financial reporting purposes.

As explained in Chapter 4, for-profit corporations are either C corporations or S corporations. Some corporations—generally those with 100 or less individual shareholders—can elect to be S corporations (under Subchapter S of the Internal Revenue Code). An S corporation generally is not subject to the income tax. Rather, its income, gains and losses flow to its shareholders for reporting by the shareholders on their personal income tax returns. All for-profit corporations that are not S corporations are C corporations. After 2017, C corporations' annual taxable income is taxed at a 21 percent rate. Prior to 2018, a graduated rate system applied to C corporations, with the highest effective rate being 35 percent.

A partnership works in a similar manner to an S corporation—its earnings and losses flow to its partners for inclusion on their personal tax returns. Generally, a limited liability company (LLC) is treated as a partnership for income tax purposes. Prior to 2018, partnerships (and

LLCs) were generally considered to be the best entity from a tax perspective, because they never pay tax and there is some flexibility to adjust allocations of the earnings, gains and losses among the business owners. In contrast, an S corporation sometimes has to pay tax and its earnings and losses must be shared by its owners pro rata based on stock holdings. After 2018, whether a C corporation is a better entity choice depends on each case's unique facts. This matter is discussed in detail in Chapter 4.

Prior to 2018, most for-profit corporations that could elect to be S corporations did so elect because an S corporation ordinarily did not, and still ordinarily does not (after 2017), have to pay income tax. C corporations are largely regulated under Subchapter C of the Internal Revenue Code. Unlike an S corporation, any person or legal entity can be a C corporation shareholder.

A C corporation is subject to tax on its taxable income. Taxable income is revenue from sales of products or services, plus other income, minus statutorily-authorized deductions. The most common deduction is permitted by Code section 162. It permits deduction of "ordinary and necessary" business expenses.

Most large companies are C corporations. The corporate income tax is anticipated to produce approximately $245 billion of federal revenue for the fiscal year ended in 2019.

Generally, all of the foregoing types of tax entities can be formed tax-free. Contributions to a corporation (whether a C or an S) upon formation ordinarily are tax-free as long as the contributors own 80 percent or more of the common stock. Contributions to partnerships and multiple member LLCs taxable as partnerships ordinarily are tax-free. Distributions of earnings from S corporations and partnerships (and LLCs taxable as partnerships) are tax-free. In contrast, a distribution of accumulated earnings from a C corporation ordinarily is subject to tax, although the capital gains rate ordinarily applies if the distributing company is a U.S. company (i.e. formed under a state's law) or a certain type of foreign corporation.

Certain affiliated C corporations (i.e. a "controlled group of corporations")—generally those eighty percent (80%) or greater affiliated through stock ownership with a common parent company, can elect to file a consolidated federal income tax return. If they do so, then intercompany transactions between affiliates generally are eliminated from the consolidated return. Only the transactions with unrelated parties produce taxable income and expense.

Trusts are separate taxpaying entities if they receive and retain income. A trust that accumulates income reaches the highest federal income tax rate (37 percent in 2019) when taxable income exceeds $12,750. For tax purposes, there are two types of trusts with respect to income accumulation: (a) those that require all of their income to be distributed each year (i.e. a simple trust); and (b) those that do not require all of their income to be distributed each year (i.e. a complex trust). As trusts are often used for asset protection, taxation of trusts is discussed in Chapter 3, Asset Protection.

Nonprofit companies often are charities or other organizations that do not attempt to profit. The Internal Revenue Code recognizes numerous types of tax-exempt entities, including governmental entities, churches, nonprofit hospitals, schools and charities. Charitable organizations are often called "501(c)(3) organizations." Under Code section 170, individual donors to 501(c)(3) organizations can take itemized tax deductions for contributions made. For other nonprofit companies (generally, those found in paragraphs of subsection c of Code section 501 other than paragraph 3), no deduction is permitted for contributions thereto. Passive earnings of 501(c)(3) organizations and other nonprofit organizations such as interest income and dividends ordinarily are tax-free to the charity. However, debt-financed income ordinarily is taxable. If a charity runs a business, it must pay tax on the business's net income in the same manner that a for-profit business would need to pay income taxes.

The income tax system applicable to individuals provides for a progressive tax rate system that is applied to a person or couple's taxable income. For 2019, the incremental rates are 10, 12, 22, 24, 32, 35 and 37 percent. For singles for 2019, the 10 rate increases to 12 percent when taxable income exceeds $9,700. For married persons filing joint returns, the rate increases from 10 to 12 percent when taxable income exceeds $19,400. The highest rate of 37 percent applies to taxable income in excess of $510,300 for single persons and $612,350 for married persons filing jointly.

A taxpayer can have a net operating loss (NOL) if business expenses exceed income. Generally, pre-2018 NOLs can be carried forward up to 20 years and post-2017 NOLs can be carried forward indefinitely and used to offset business net income in future years. When carried forward, their use is limited to 80 percent of the net income in year of carryforward.

Income. For individuals, taxable income is the excess of income over allowed deductions, and it is also whatever Congress says it is. Over the years, Congress has made many changes to the system—particularly to the deduction piece of the system. However, some deductions have experienced relatively little change.

Income is, generally speaking, any addition to wealth produced by something other than a gift or a bequest. Virtually all income is taxable unless a statutory exemption applies. Many statutory exemptions exist, particularly in the area of employee benefits. Contributions by an employee or an employer to a cafeteria plan for various benefits generally are tax-free to the employee and tax-deductible to the employer. Up to a limit ($2,700 for 2019), these amounts include amounts contributed to a flexible spending account (FSA) that can be used on a tax-free basis to pay out-of-pocket medical expenses. Employer contributions to "tax-qualified" retirement plans are not taxable to employees. Rather, only upon distribution of funds are employees taxed. Even then, employees ordinarily can "roll over" benefits to an IRA or another tax-qualified plan on a tax-free basis for further tax-free growth. (As discussed in Chapter 8, a tax-qualified plan is one that meets the requirements of Internal Revenue Code section 401(a).)

Up to $5,250 of education benefits and up to $5,000 of dependent care assistance can be supplied to employees by employers on a tax-free basis. A large exclusion (generally, up to $14,080) exists for employer-supplied adoption benefits. Lawsuit recoveries generally are taxable, except for amounts paid to reimburse for physical injuries.

Generally, interest income is taxable. However, income from state and local government bonds generally is tax-free. Income on U.S. government bonds is taxable by the federal government, but not by state or local governments.

Refunds of state income taxes are taxable unless no tax benefit was produced by payment of the state income tax. Federal income tax refunds are not taxable by the federal government.

Life insurance proceeds ordinarily are received free of income tax. However, no deduction is permitted for purchase of a policy (i.e. for policy premium payments). Certain policy transfers can cause the transferee to have to recognize gain or loss with respect to a policy's benefits. Disability income received from a disability income insurance policy generally is taxable if deductions were taken for the premium payments, and tax-free if no deductions were taken for the premium payments. Many forms of compensation paid to veterans are tax-free.

If an individual is in debt and his debt is discharged, income generally must be recognized due to the discharge because the person's net worth increases. However, a number of exceptions exist. If one of certain exceptions applies (i.e. insolvency, bankruptcy and certain farm debt), favorable tax attributes (e.g. the depreciable basis of assets, net operating losses) generally must be reduced by the amount of income that was not required to be recognized. Also, if a student loan provides that debt will be eliminated for working in a certain profession for a certain period of time for one of any of a broad class of employers, discharge of debt income is not recognized if the work is done, or it is not done due to death or total and permanent disability.

Stock or other equity received from an employer is taxable income. However, a stock option ordinarily does not produce income until the stock option is exercised. Then, the income is the excess of the value of the stock over the purchase price. Certain options—incentive stock options (ISOs)—do not produce income when exercised and the ultimate gain later received upon sale of the stock is capital gain. TCJA added a deferral mechanism for certain stock options that are made available to large portion of a company's employees. It seems few companies will adopt such a plan.

Capital Gains and Losses. Capital gains are subject to their own tax regime, with gains and losses netted, and net gains relating to capital assets held more than one year (i.e. long-term capital gains) being subject to a relatively low tax rate (ranging from 0 to 20 percent). Short-term gains and losses relate to assets held less than a year. If a net capital loss exists, only $3,000 of it can be "taken" during the year, and the remainder is carried forward indefinitely. While a lower tax rate applies to net long-term capital gain income than the rate applicable to other (ordinary) income, net short-term capital gains produce no benefit (i.e. they are treated as ordinary income). Generally, for married individuals filing jointly for 2019, up to $78,749 of net long-term capital gain is tax-free, net gain in excess of $78,749 but not in excess of $488,849 is subject to tax at a 15 percent rate, and net gain in excess of $488,849 is taxed at a 20 percent rate. For single taxpayers, the cut-offs are $39,374 and $434,539.

Dividends from domestic corporations and certain foreign corporations are eligible for capital gains tax rates. Generally, dividends from foreign corporations are "qualified" if the U.S. has a tax treaty with the country of origin that provides for free exchange of tax information or the corporation's stock is publicly-traded on a U.S. exchange. Tax calculation is more complex if such "qualified dividends" exist.

For individuals, a gain is the excess of the amount realized upon the sale of a piece of property over the adjusted basis of the property. The amount realized includes cash and other property received in a sale, and it ordinarily includes any debt assumed by the buyer, including debt secured by the property. The adjusted basis of a piece of property ordinarily is its original cost. Adjusted basis can be increased if capital improvements, etc. are added to the asset. For example, an addition of a garage to a house would increase the house's adjusted basis. A loss ordinarily is the excess of the adjusted basis of a piece of property over the amount realized on sale. Depreciation deductions reduce an asset's adjusted basis. There are some special rules that defer or eliminate taxation with respect to certain gains, such as a like-kind exchange. However, losses from personal-use property (e.g. a car not used for business) are not deductible.

Long-term capital gains and losses, relating to capital assets held more than a year, are netted to determine if a net long-term capital gain or a net long-term capital loss exists. The same applies to short-term capital gains and losses. (A net long-term capital gain is the excess of long-term capital gains over long-term capital losses. The opposite is true for net losses. A net short-term capital gain is the excess of short-term capital gains over short-term capital losses. The opposite is true for net losses.) An excess of net long-term capital gain over a net short-term capital loss is subject to the preferential capital gains rates. If both a net long-term capital gain exists and a net short-term capital gain exists, the long-term gain is subject to preferred rates while the net short-term gain is taxable as ordinary income. If both a net short-term capital loss and a net long-term capital loss exist, they are deductible against ordinary income up to the $3,000 limitation, with the excess carried forward. The same applies if a net long-term capital loss exceeds a net short-term capital gain, or if a net short-term capital loss exceeds a net long-term capital gain.

Capital gains and losses exist only with respect to capital assets. Generally speaking, a capital asset is any property other than inventory, supplies, depreciable property such as equipment, intellectual property such as a copyright and accounts receivable. Perhaps the most common capital asset is company stock. Land generally is a capital asset. While a personal residence is a capital asset, generally, a single person may exclude up to $250,000 gain upon the sale of a personal residence. For married persons filing jointly, the amount that generally can be excluded is $500,000. (Conditions exist for the exclusion to apply.) While depreciable property is not a capital asset, its disposition can sometimes produce capital gain.

The 2017 tax act created a means of deferring or even eliminating long-term capital gain by investing proceeds of an investment in a business that largely operates in a "qualified opportunity zone" (QOZ). A QOZ is a population census tract that is a low-income community as designated by the CEO of a state and certified by the IRS as accepted. Generally, the longer the investment is held, the more potential gain is reduced and, if held 10 years or more, the gain disappears. These type arrangements have been in the tax laws in various iterations over the years.

Under Code §1202, taxpayers other than corporations can sell stock of certain C corporations completely tax-free. The stock can potentially be owned by a pass-through entity, including an S corporation. Only certain business types potentially qualify. Professional practices, banks, motels, restaurants and farms generally don't qualify. Five year holding and active business requirements generally apply. The stock must be original issue stock. The gain is generally limited to $10 million. Gross assets upon formation cannot exceed $50 million. As most business sales are asset sales, this benefit will have limited value.

Depreciable assets as well as real estate held and used in a trade or business will generally produce capital gain if sold at a gain, but an ordinary loss if sold at a loss. Some property doesn't qualify, including real estate held as inventory (which would not be capital gain property) and property held less than a year. Also, all depreciation recapture (discussed below) is ordinary income. Gains and losses on qualifying business assets are netted, and the net is either treated as long-term capital gain if it is a gain or an ordinary loss if it is a loss. (This treatment is provided for by section 1231 of the Code.)

Generally, if an asset other than inventory or accounts receivable is sold and payment for it will be received over two or more years, then any gain can be recognized in installments over the anticipated years of payments. If interest is not required with the payments or the interest charged is insufficient based on statutory rates, interest may need to be "imputed." In other words, part of the payments for an asset might be need to be treated as interest income instead of as part of the amount received relating to the sale of the asset.

If property held for investment or for use in a trade or business is exchanged solely for "like-kind" property to be held for investment or use in a trade or business, then any gain in the asset being exchanged is not recognized. Instead, it is deferred through a "carryover" of its adjusted basis to the asset received in the exchange. However, if cash or "boot" is also received, then gain recognition exists up to the amount of the cash or boot. This rule, found in Code section 1031, does not apply to inventory or investments such as common stock or a promissory note. After 2017, under TCJA, section 1031 applies only to real estate held as an investment or used in a business.

Some capitalized assets such as land cannot be depreciated. Those assets that can be depreciated are subject to depreciation using a method and time span that is set by statute. Some assets (e.g. a computer) have a much shorter depreciable life than other assets (e.g. a building). Generally speaking, real estate is subject to depreciation over the longest term. It is 27.5 years for residential real estate and 39 years for commercial real estate. Only the physical building or structure on land is subject to depreciation. So, when land with a building or other structure on it is purchased, the purchase price must be apportioned between land and the structure(s), based on relative values. Depreciable real estate is subject to "straight line" depreciation (i.e. equal amounts over the depreciation time span), but other shorter life assets can often be subjected to an accelerated depreciation method where more depreciation is taken in the earlier years of ownership.

Congress provides for "expensing" of capital asset purchases when it wishes to create economic incentive for people to buy capital assets. Since the early days of the Great Recession, Congress has allowed very significant expensing of capital asset purchases. In 2019, under section 179, up to $1,020,000 of most capital asset purchases other than real estate can be expensed by small businesses, provided the expense cannot produce a net loss. Some commercial real estate related improvement purchases qualify. The ability to deduct phases out once purchases total $2,550,000.

Under Code section 168(k), in 2019, the full cost of machinery and equipment and certain other assets can be expensed in the year of purchase. For these purposes, unlike prior to 2018, it does not matter if the property is new or used.

Subject to a $25,500 section 179 limit on SUVs and certain other vehicles, generally, vehicles are eligible for expensing. However, Code section 280F places limits on depreciation of passenger cars. When expensing applies, the first year limit is $18,000. Thereafter, the annual limit is $16,000 for year 2, $9,600 for year 3 and $5,760 for later years. Passenger vehicles with respect to which expensing is not elected are subject to deduction limits of $10,000, $16,000, $9,600 and $5,760 for the first, second, third, and fourth and later years of ownership.

Code section 280F also limits depreciation deductions on property that has the ability to be used for personal purposes, as well as for business purposes, called "listed property." A personal computer is listed property. Basically, such property must be used predominantly for business in order for ordinary depreciation benefits to apply (including section 179). The depreciation is based on the percentage of the asset that is used for business. If the property is used 50 percent or less for business purposes, a less beneficial depreciation method must be used. Also, if the asset was originally used predominantly for business but its business use percent later drops to 50 percent or less, then depreciation recapture takes place to the degree the depreciation taken exceeds that which would have applied under the less beneficial system, and the less beneficial system applies thereafter.

Since large expensing is permitted under both Code section 179 and 168(k), the question arises as to which one is best to use. Section 179 can be applied on an asset-by-asset basis, whereas section 168(k) must be applied on an asset class basis. Recapture applies under both sections if business use drops below 50 percent. Some commercial real estate related improvements can qualify under section 179, but not under section 168(k). Section 168(k) can create a loss; section 179 cannot do so.

If a depreciated asset is sold, then the gain upon the sale (if any) generally results in depreciation "recapture" to the extent of certain depreciation previously taken. The recaptured amount is ordinary income. For machinery and equipment, and for real property held less than a year, all of the depreciation previously taken is potentially subject to recapture. So, for example, if a piece of machinery with a tax basis of $1,000,000 is sold three years after purchase for $1,800,000, and $500,000 of depreciation was previously taken (such that the original cost was $1,500,000), then $500,000 of the $800,000 gain would be ordinary income. These rules override the installment gain recognition rules (discussed herein), such that recapture income is recognized in the year of sale.

Deductions. Like income, deductions pose complexities for individuals, along with the additional need to determine whether capitalization is required. The individual income tax system recognizes two categories of deductions: "above-the-line" or "for AGI" deductions and "below-the-line" or itemized deductions. Above-the-line deductions are deductions that anyone can take. The sum of a taxpayer's income minus above-the-line deductions produces Adjusted Gross Income, or "AGI." AGI is important because many tax benefits, including deductions and credits, turn on AGI or a derivative thereof. The same is true for certain entitlements, as well as Obamacare premium credits and subsidies.

Sometimes limitations on deductions exist. Above-the-line deductions reduce taxable income. The following above-the-line deductions are the ones most commonly taken:

- IRA contributions
- Half of the self-employment tax (for self-employed persons)
- Health savings account (HSA) contributions
- Tax-qualified plan contributions by self-employed persons
- Health insurance premiums of self-employed persons

- Student loan interest (subject to limits—generally, $2,500 with a phase-out beginning when AGI exceeds $70,000 if single/$140,000 if married filing jointly).

Other above-the-line deductions include educator expenses and certain moving expenses of military personnel.

For self-employed persons, significant potential above-the-line deductions exist. These include deductions to tax-qualified retirement plans or a simplified employee pension (SEP), premiums for health insurance that cover the person and possibly his/her family, health savings account (HSA) contributions if the person also participates in a high deductible health plan and one-half of the self-employment tax. The HSA deductible limits for 2019 are $3,500 for self-only coverage and $7,000 for family coverage. An additional $1,000 "catch-up" contribution is available if age 55 or greater by year-end.

Subject to limits that increase with age (specified in the following paragraph), as specified in Code section 213(d), self-employed persons can deduct long-term care premiums. For this purpose, as is the case with many Code sections, partners, LLC members and two-percent or greater S corporation shareholders are treated as self-employed persons.

Itemized deductions are deductions that produce tax reduction only if the aggregate of them exceeds the "standard deduction." For 2019, the standard deduction is $12,200 for single persons, $18,350 for heads of households and $24,400 for married taxpayers filing jointly. For married persons who are disabled or age 65 or greater, an additional $1,300 of standard deduction applies. For single taxpayers and heads of households who are disabled or age 65 or greater, an additional $1,650 of standard deduction applies.

The most commonly taken itemized deductions are state and local income or sales taxes, property taxes, home mortgage interest and charitable contributions. TCJA limits the deductibility of state and local taxes to $10,000. Note: TCJA substantially increased the standard deduction. By doing so, it made itemizing deductions unappealing to a large segment of Americans.

Medical expenses are deductible as itemized deductions only if and to the extent they exceed a percentage of AGI. For 2019, the percentage is 10.0. Medical expenses include health insurance premiums and, to a limited degree, long-term care premiums. For 2019, premiums for long-term care can be deducted up to $420 if age 40 or less, $790 if greater than age 40 but not more than 50, $1,580 if greater than age 50 but not more than 60, $4,220 if greater than age 60 but not more than age 70, and $5,270 if greater than age 70.

There are limits on charitable deductions, with contributions to churches, governmental units, schools, and public charities (including nonprofit hospitals) generally being limited to 60 percent of AGI and contributions to private "nonoperating" foundations generally being limited to the lesser of the 50 percent of AGI minus public charity contributions or 30 percent of AGI. (TCJA increased the limit relating to churches, governmental units, schools and public charities from 50 percent to 60 percent.) A donation of capital gain property to a church, governmental unit, school or public charity is subject to a 30 percent of AGI limit, unless only the adjusted basis of the property is deducted. A five year carryforward applies to nondeductible amounts. No deduction is permitted for political contributions or lobbying expenditures.

Whether interest expense can be deducted depends on the type of interest expense. Interest on credit cards and other personal interest expense is not deductible. Under TCJA, interest incurred in a trade or business ordinarily is deductible up to the sum of (1) interest income; (2) floor plan financing interest income; and (3) 30 percent of adjusted taxable income. Floor plan financing interest generally is interest incurred to finance vehicles for sale. Adjusted taxable income has a specific meaning, and generally excludes deductions for depreciation, amortization and depletion (relating to oil and gas, etc.). The foregoing limit on trade or business interest does not apply if the taxpayer's gross receipts have averaged $25 million or less during the prior three-year period.

Interest on home mortgage debt incurred after 2017 to purchase, build or improve a home and possibly a second home is deductible with respect to a maximum of $750,000 of debt. A $1,000,000 limit generally exists with respect to a mortgage taken or agreed upon prior to December 15, 2017. After 2017, interest on a home equity line of credit (HELOC) is not deductible. Prior to 2018, HELOC interest was generally deductible on up to $100,000 of principal. Investment interest incurred to purchase or carry an investment generally can be deducted up to net investment income. Refinanced debts ordinarily receive the same treatment as the original debt. Other rules apply to passive activity debt. (Passive loss rules are discussed below.)

Prior to 2018, personal exemptions also reduced taxable income. However, TCJA eliminated personal exemptions. Also after 2017, entertainment expenses cannot be deducted at all. However, 50 percent of business meals with clients/customers can be deducted.

Retirement Contributions. Saving for retirement ordinarily produces tax deductions for individuals and companies. Retirement assets and their earnings ordinarily grow tax-free. Distributions from tax-qualified plans (i.e. pension, 401(k) and profit-sharing plans) and IRAs are, almost always, taxable as ordinary income. (An exception can exist for company stock distributed from a tax-qualified plan.) In addition to income tax, a ten percent (10%) penalty applies to distributions taken prior to attainment of age 59½, unless the distribution is taken due to death, disability or one of a few other reasons. However, distributable amounts can be "rolled over" tax-free to another IRA or possibly even another tax-qualified plan. Retirement plans are discussed in Chapter 8.

For 2019, generally, any working individual can contribute the lesser of their earned income or $6,000 to an IRA. For this purpose, earned income generally includes alimony. If the person will be age 50 or older at year-end, an additional $1,000 "catch up" contribution can be made. Such contributions generally are tax-deductible for income tax purposes. However, to be tax-deductible for a year, an IRA contribution must be made by April 15th of the following year. Excess contributions are not deductible and are generally subject to a six percent excise tax.

The ability to deduct a contribution can potentially be diminished or lost with respect to a person who actively participates in a tax-qualified plan of his employer if the person's income (or the joint income of the person and his or her spouse, if married and a joint return will be filed) exceeds a certain threshold. Generally speaking, a person actively participates in a tax-qualified plan for a year if he makes a contribution to the plan or receives a benefit increase under the plan. For a joint return, generally (subject to income limits), the spouse of a person who participates in a tax-qualified plan can contribute $6,000 (plus another $1,000 if age 50 or older) to an IRA on a tax-deductible basis.

A single person who actively participates in a tax-qualified plan can deduct the lesser of the contribution limit ($6,000 or $7,000 for 2019) or the deduction limit amount. The deduction limit amount phases out for 2019 with respect to modified adjusted gross income (MAGI) between $64,000 and $74,000. (So, $74,000 of MAGI is the deduction limit, and a deductible IRA contribution cannot be made by a single person who is an active participant.) For the vast majority, MAGI is AGI.

If both spouses of a married couple that files a joint return actively participate in tax-qualified plans, the ability to make deductible contributions phases out between AGI of $103,000 and $123,000 for 2019. (The phase-out applies to the $6,000 or $7,000 contribution limit.) The lesser paid active participant spouse can deduct the lesser of the contribution limit, as adjusted due to the AGI active participation limit, or the sum of the compensation of the lesser paid spouse and the compensation of the higher paid spouse minus the combination of any IRA deduction for the higher paid spouse, the amount of designated nondeductible IRA contributions by the higher paid spouse and any Roth IRA contributions by the higher paid spouse. If only one spouse of a couple that files jointly actively participates in a tax-qualified plan, the ability of the other spouse to make a tax-deductible contribution phases out between $193,000 and $203,000 of MAGI. The other spouse need not have earned compensation to able to make such an IRA contribution.

Elective deferrals to 401(k) plans other than Roth elective deferrals reduce an employee's Form W-2 income that is subject to income tax. However, FICA taxes (discussed below) are not reduced by such contributions. Roth contributions reduce neither income tax nor FICA tax. Cafeteria plan contributions are excluded form W-2 and FICA income.

Miscellaneous Deductions. Sometimes, assets are involuntarily converted via things such as a storm or eminent domain. In such cases, generally, if cash received is invested in property similar to the property destroyed or taken within a specified time frame, no gain is recognized. Otherwise, gain must be recognized up to the amount of cash received and not reinvested. TCJA eliminated deductibility of casualty losses unless the casualty is incurred in a presidentially-declared national disaster area.

Business use of a personal automobile by a self-employed person gives rise to a tax deduction. Expenses are aggregated and then the total cost apportioned between personal and business use. Limitations potentially apply to depreciation and leasing costs. Alternatively, a taxpayer can use the automatic mileage method, whereby a deduction is given for each business mile driven. The IRS annually supplies the cost per mile. For 2019, the rate is 58 cents per mile. In addition, parking charges and fees can be deducted. A 14 cent rate applies to miles driven for charity. A 20 cent rate applies to medical travel.

Persons who are self-employed and use part of their home exclusively for business purposes can deduct a part of the total costs relating to the home, including depreciation, utilities, taxes and repairs. Alternatively, a deduction of $5 per square foot can be utilized. Limitations exist.

Prior to 2018, employees could take itemized deductions for unreimbursed business expenses, investment expenses and tax preparation fees to the extent that they exceeded two percent (2%) of AGI. Numerous other potential itemized deductions were also subject to the two percent limit, including investment expenses. After 2017, these deductions no longer exist. Some states may still permit them.

After 2018, alimony and child support payments are not deductible by the payer and are not income to the payee.

Loss Limitations. Limitations exist throughout the Code on the ability of taxpayers to take losses. Under Code section 465, taxpayers generally can take deductions only for the amounts they are "at risk" with respect to a sole proprietorship, partnership, LLC or S corporation. Generally, a taxpayer is at risk with respect to amounts loaned to the entity, amounts contributed to the entity (with the adjusted basis of contributed property counted) and debts of the entity guaranteed by the taxpayer.

In addition to the at risk rules, under Code sections 704(d) and 1366(d), members of multiple member LLCs, partners of partnerships and shareholders of S corporations can only take losses up to the amount of their adjusted basis of their equity interest for loss purposes. With respect to multiple member LLCs and partnerships, owners generally have adjusted basis for loss purposes to the extent of their equity interest (i.e. adjusted basis of capital contributions plus earnings share, minus losses share and distributions) plus their share of the debts of the entity for which: (a) they are directly or indirectly personally liable; or (b) no one is personally liable. For an S corporation, a shareholder generally has adjusted basis for loss purposes equal to his equity interest (i.e. adjusted basis of capital contributions plus earnings share, minus losses share and distributions) plus amounts directly loaned to the corporation.

The passive loss rules of Code section 469 further limit the ability of partners in partnerships, members of multiple member LLCs and shareholders of S corporations to take "passive" losses "passed through" by the business entity. Generally, if the owner does not "materially participate" in the business, his or her loss share is passive in nature, and it cannot be deducted except to offset passive income of any business activity or future profits of the entity. Passive losses of the taxpayer are netted with passive profits (of other entities wholly or partially owned by the taxpayer), and the losses taken to the extent of the profits. Losses not taken are carried forward to the next year. In the year of disposition of an interest in an entity, any remaining suspended loss relating to that entity can be deducted.

For purposes of the passive loss rules, "material participation" generally means work activity that is regular, continuous and substantial. If person works more than 500 hours during a year with respect to an activity, the activity is not a passive activity (and any losses with respect to it are not limited due to the passive loss rules). Numerous other means of avoiding passive activity status exist. However, generally, any real estate activity is a passive activity. A few exceptions exist, including one for active participation by certain taxpayers whose AGI doesn't exceed a threshold.

Under Code section 267, losses on sales between related taxpayers generally are disallowed, but any future gain experienced by the buyer is reduced by the foregone loss. However, with respect to a controlled group of corporations filing a consolidated tax return, the loss is (instead) suspended until the property is sold to a third party. Also under Code section 267, if a person (including a company) would ordinarily be allowed a deduction with respect to a transaction with a related person, and the related person would ordinarily not recognize income until a later year, then the deduction is deferred until income is recognized by the related person.

Foreigners. Foreign citizens residing outside the U.S. and foreign companies (i.e. those formed and maintained under non-U.S. law) generally pay federal income tax only on their U.S. source income, including dividends received from U.S. companies. Foreign individuals and companies must be engaged in a trade or business in the U.S. (ETB) in order for them to be subject to U.S. taxation on their U.S. trade or business net income. U.S. tax rates apply to such net income. Foreigners are generally subject to tax at a 30 percent rate on their fixed and other determinable periodic income from U.S. sources, including dividends and interest paid by U.S. corporations. Foreigners who are not present in the U.S. ordinarily do not pay tax on capital gains with respect to U.S. assets, including stock held in U.S. companies. An exception exists for U.S. real estate.

U.S. citizens and residents (regardless of their citizenship), pay tax on their worldwide income. However, individuals are entitled to a tax credit for foreign source income that is limited to the tax the U.S. would have levied on the income. For example, if $1,000,000 of earnings of a U.S. citizen was in a foreign country that applied a 40 percent tax rate (i.e. $400,000 of tax) while the U.S. applied a 35 percent tax rate, a $350,000 credit would be available. In contrast, if the foreign rate was 20 percent (and $200,000 of foreign tax was paid), the credit would be $200,000. Under an exception to the worldwide inclusion and tax credit system, certain individuals working abroad for an extended period of time can exclude up to $105,900 earned while working abroad in 2019.

Under Code section 482, the IRS can adjust transfer prices, profits and deductions, etc. of transactions between two or more organizations, trades or businesses under common control when the prices applied are not "arm's length" in nature. This Code section is often used by the IRS to adjust transactions involving international operations of businesses.

Tax treaties can override the above rules. The U.S. has tax treaties with many, but far from all, countries.

Tax Filings. An annual income tax return is filed to report income and deductions. Form 1040 is the common income tax return for individuals. Simpler returns can use an abridged form (e.g. 1040A). C corporations file Form 1120. S corporations file Form 1120S. Partnerships and multiple member LLCs treated as partnerships for income tax purposes file Form 1065. Sole proprietorships and single member LLCs report their net income or loss on Schedule C of Form 1040 of the business owner.

Various businesses must report payments and receipts with respect to many taxpayers, making only the cash part of the system not traceable by the IRS. For example, using Form W-2, employers report to the IRS their employees' wages and other pertinent tax information. Using Form 1098, mortgage lenders report to the IRS and mortgage payers the mortgage payments made the by taxpayer(s). Using Form 1099, brokerage companies report dividends, interest, capital asset disposition income and gain/loss.

There was a time when assets could be placed in the name of children, who were in a lower tax bracket due to the progressive nature of the income tax system, to produce household savings. However, the "kiddie tax" largely eliminates this saving device. In 2019, the (highly progressive) tax rate system applicable to estates and trusts applies to the unearned income of a child under the age of 19, or under the age of 24 if a dependent full-time student with a living parent.

Coverdell education savings accounts and 529 accounts (i.e. covered by Code section 529) are means of allowing tax-free growth of assets for education purposes. TCJA greatly increased the appeal of 529 accounts, by permitting per-beneficiary distributions of $10,000 per year for elementary and secondary school tuition and costs. The limit applies regardless of the number of 529 accounts that exist for the beneficiary. So, at least after 2017, 529 accounts are the more appealing of the two options. They are thoroughly discussed in Chapter 7, Federal Financial Aid for College.

Subject to tweaks and changes recently made by the TCJA, the federal income tax system described above has been in existence for many decades. The Tax Reform Act of 1986 lowered the tax rates, reduced deductions and increased capitalization requirements. In other words, it looked good from a political perspective (lower rates) but produced roughly the same amount of revenue by cutting back deductions while making the system more complex. TCJA eliminated some benefits while adding or expanding others.

TCJA 20 Percent Deduction. TCJA added a new substantial deduction for trades or businesses conducted by individuals (including through a single member LLC), S corporations and partnerships (including LLCs treated as partnerships for federal tax purposes). Generally, under new Code section 199A, 20 percent of the net taxable income of the trades or businesses can be taken as a deduction for income tax purposes. If a net loss exists, it is carried forward. The deduction can be taken whether or not the taxpayer itemizes deductions, but it does not reduce AGI. And, subject to a large exemption, it does not apply to most professional services income because a professional service is not a "qualified trade or business." Exceptions exist for engineering and architecture. Also excluded from the definition of a "qualified trade or business" are brokerage and asset management services.

The deduction can potentially be less than 20 percent of the net taxable income. The deduction applicable to most taxpayers is the lesser of the "combined qualified business income amount" of the qualified businesses in which the taxpayer has business activity or 20 percent of the excess of taxable income over net capital gain. For most taxpayers, the combined qualified business income amount is the sum of the following "qualified business income" (QBI) amounts determined separately with respect to each qualified trade or business carried on: The lesser of (a) 20 percent of the QBI of the trade or business; or (b) the greater of (i) 50 percent of the W-2 wages paid with respect to the qualified trade or business, and (ii) the sum of 25 percent of W-2 wages with respect to the qualified trade or business plus 2.5 percent of the unadjusted basis of all qualified property of the trade or business. Generally, qualified property is depreciable property used in the business that has not been owned longer than the greater of ten years or the property's depreciable life. Exceptions to the preceding rule follow. (Note: For all section 199A calculation purposes, taxable income is computed without the section 199A deduction.)

The 50 percent of W-2 wages/25 percent of W-2 wages plus 2.5 percent, etc. provision does not apply if the taxpayer's taxable income does not exceed the threshold amount for year. Instead, the 20 percent amount applies.

The threshold amount for 2019 for married taxpayers filing jointly is $321,400; for everyone else, it is $160,700. Also, if the 50 percent of W-2 wages/25 percent of W-2 wages plus 2.5 percent, etc. amount is less than the 20 percent amount and taxable income exceeds the threshold amount by less than the phase-out amount, then the 20 percent deduction will apply, but it will be reduced by the excess of the 20 percent amount over the 50 percent of W-2 wages/25 percent of W-2 wages plus 2.5 percent, etc. amount, pro rata for taxable income in excess of the threshold. The phase-out amount is $100,000 for married persons filing jointly, and $50,000 for everyone else. An example follows.

Assume a single taxpayer with $190,700 of taxable income exclusive of capital gain has one qualified trade or business which: (a) had QBI of $200,000: (b) paid W-2 wages of $40,000; and (c) had qualified property with an unadjusted basis of $100,000. Prior to the reduction noted in the preceding paragraph, the 20 percent amount would be $40,000 (i.e. 200,000 x .2). The greater of the 50 percent of W-2 wages amount and 25 percent of W-2 wages and 2.5 percent, etc. amount would be the greater of $20,000 (i.e. 40,000 x .5) and $12,500 (i.e. (.25 x 40,000) + (100,000 x .025). The excess of $40,000 over the greater amount of $20,000 would be $20,000. As taxable income is $30,000 over the threshold amount of $160,700 and the phase-out amount is $50,000, the reduction percent is 60 (i.e. (190,700-160,700)/50,000)). Applying .60 to the difference of $20,000 produces a $12,000 reduction to the $40,000 amount, causing the deduction to be $28,000.

With respect to a qualified trade or business, QBI is the net of its income, gain, deduction and loss from U.S. operations. Passive income, including dividends, is not included. Also excluded is "reasonable compensation" paid to the taxpayer by the qualified trade or business, including any compensation paid to a partner or member in the entity for services falling within the definition of Code section 707(c) (i.e. guaranteed payments). The rules apply to S corporations and partnerships (including LLCs treated as partnerships) at the shareholder/partner/member level, meaning each shareholder/partner/member takes into account his or her share of the income, gain, deduction and loss, as well as the allocable W-2 wages, etc., of the business entity.

Final regulations and related IRS notices were issued in early 2019 with respect to the new 20 percent deduction. Concerning compensation paid to S corporation shareholders and guaranteed payments to members of an LLC (or partners in a partnership), the final regulations require that such amounts reduce QBI. Retirement plan contributions also reduce QBI. An example of how the QBI deduction impacts retirement plan contributions is provided in Chapter 8.

Professional services and brokerage or asset management services that ordinarily would not qualify because the service performed is not a qualified trade or business will qualify if the taxpayer's taxable income for the year does not exceed the threshold amount (specified above). If taxable income exceeds the threshold amount but not by more than the phase-out amount (also specified above), the deduction is phased-out to the extent taxable income exceeds the threshold but does not exceed the sum of the threshold amount and the phase-out amount, in a manner similar to the manner shown by the preceding example with respect to a single taxpayer.

The 2019 final regulations and a related notice produced a relatively easy standard for real estate activities to potentially qualify for the QBI deduction. Provided 250 or more hours of rental-related work (such as repairs, renting, maintenance, etc. but not investment management activities) are performed by one or more persons with respect to a real estate enterprise (that could include more than one property), and solid contemporaneous records are kept of hours and work done, the activity potentially qualifies.

One legal entity (e.g. an LLC) or multiple legal entities could own multiple qualified trades or businesses. Provided done consistently and certain conditions are met, these entities can be aggregated for purposes of computing the deduction. Also, trades or businesses that are split between two or more legal entities (e.g. a physician practice and an office building) generally can be aggregated. Expenses that benefit more than one trade or business must be apportioned among the business in a reasonable manner.

Losses that are suspended under the loss limitation rules discussed elsewhere in this chapter (including Code sections 465, 469, 704(d) and 1366(d)) are carried forward and applied in later years when they can be taken under the loss limitation rules. However, pre-2018 losses are not taken into account.

The new tax regime breeds new life into an old tax— the accumulated earnings tax. This 20 percent tax, found in Code sections 531-537, applies to C corporations that accumulate earnings beyond the reasonable needs of the business. With the new low 21 percent tax rate on C corporations and potential low capital gains rates for individuals, some companies might remain a C corporation, or elect to be taxed as a C corporation, and defer distributions or stretch distributions over many years to produce an end result that is better than the result that would exist if pass-through status had existed for the entity. Generally, the IRS must audit and propose assessment of the tax for exposure to exist. For most people reading this book, it will be better to maintain a pass-through entity (generally, an LLC or S corporation).

State and Local Taxes. State and local governments often levy income taxes as well. A typical rate is in the range of 6 percent. Some states have much higher income tax rates (e.g. California), and some states (e.g. Florida) have no income tax. States also have sales and use taxes. States that do not have an income tax generally have a sales and use tax rate that is greater than the sales and use tax rate of states levying income taxes. Otherwise, the shortfall is made up somewhere. State taxable income ordinarily is defined as federal taxable income, plus and minus certain adjustments. States have various ways of taxing part-year residents and nonresidents owning pass-through interests (via LLCs, etc.) of businesses operating within their boundaries.

The FICA & Medicare Tax. The FICA tax, like the income tax, produces a substantial amount of federal revenue. For the 2019 fiscal year of the federal government, combined with the self-employment (SECA) tax, the FICA tax is anticipated to produce $1,180 trillion of revenue—34 percent of total federal revenue.

The FICA tax is relatively simple with respect to employees. For Social Security, employers withhold 6.2 percent of each employee's wages up to the "Social Security Wage Base," then match this amount, and send the money to the U.S. Treasury to fund Social Security benefits. The Social Security Wage Base has gradually increased over time for inflation. For 2019, the amount is $132,900. The Medicare tax also applies equally to employee and employer (and is withheld from wages by the employer), except the rate is 1.45 percent and there is no income cap. An additional 0.9 percent tax applies to wages in excess of

$200,000 and $250,000 for single persons and married persons filing jointly, respectively.

For self-employed persons, through the Self-Employed Contributions Act (SECA), the FICA tax and the Medicare tax apply as if they were both employer and employee. Accordingly, a 12.4 percent tax applies to income up to the Social Security Wage Base to fund the Social Security trust fund, and a 2.9 percent Medicare tax applies to all self-employment income. The 0.9 percent tax also applies. The tax base is reduced by one-half of the (tentatively) computed tax, and the tax is then computed. Unlike employees, with respect to whom gross wages are subject to the combined tax, only the net business income of self-employed persons is subject to tax. The combined FICA tax and Medicare tax with respect to self-employed persons is sometimes called either the self-employment tax or SECA tax. While employees are subject to income, FICA and Medicare tax withholding, self-employed persons pay their income, FICA and Medicare taxes by making quarterly payments to the IRS.

Once the Social Security Wage Base is reached for the year, the Social Security tax does not apply for the remainder of the year. If the tax is overpaid, either because of working for more than one employer or because of being both employed and self-employed, the excess tax is recovered through the taxpayer's Form 1040 filing.

Ordinary and necessary business expenses of self-employed persons can be deducted from income in computing the SECA tax. However, unlike the income tax system, non-business expenses such as retirement plan contributions and HSA contributions are not deductible. One-half of self-employment income is deductible for income tax purposes. Passive income, including real estate income, ordinarily is not subject to the tax.

The AMT. The alternative minimum tax (AMT) is a tax system in itself. The AMT applies if the preliminary tax attributable to the AMT exceeds the tax computed under the ordinary income tax system. Basically, tax preferences, certain items excluded from income such as certain interest on state and local government bonds and certain other deductions of the ordinary tax system that are deemed by Congress to be excessive (but not too excessive to be apply to the ordinary tax system) must be added back to taxable income. Then, a significant exemption (for 2019, $111,700 for married taxpayers filing jointly and $71,700 for all others) is applied and a 26 or 28 percent tax rate is applied to compute the preliminary AMT. The exemption amount phases out beginning at $1,020,600 of alternative minimum taxable income for married taxpayers filing jointly and at $510,300 for all others. From the AMT figure is subtracted the ordinary income tax to produce the AMT. The AMT is then added to the ordinary tax to produce the tax liability. Some credits may reduce the tax.

Obamacare's 3.8 Percent Tax. Obamacare added a new 3.8 percent tax on investment income for upper middle income and above taxpayers. With it came hundreds of pages of regulations.

For individuals, the 3.8 percent tax applies to the lesser of net investment income for the year or the excess of modified adjusted gross income over a threshold amount. For single persons and persons filing as head of household, the threshold amount is $200,000. For married persons filing a joint return, the threshold amount is $250,000. Modified AGI generally means AGI. (An adjustment is needed if foreign earned income exists from work in a foreign country.)

Net investment income means investment income minus related expenses. Investment income includes interest, dividends, annuities, royalties and rents other than such income derived in the ordinary course of a trade or business. Also included are net capital gains. The "net" in net investment income is where the complexity and the hundreds of pages of regulations come into play. Deductions are permitted to the extent "properly allocable to such gross income or net gain."

Estate and Gift Tax. As this book is targeted at individuals and households making $75,000 to $400,000 per year and the estate and gift tax exemption is $11,400,000 in 2019, presumably few readers of this book will have estate or gift tax concerns. The estate and gift tax is a combined system, such that the tax applies to lifetime and at death transfers. Prior transfers during life are added to property passing at death to determine the gross amount that has transferred. Then, deductions are applied. If the net exceeds $11.4 million, an estate tax is payable. However, using portability (discussed below), married persons can pass up to double the $11.4 million exemption amount free of tax.

The annual exclusion for gifts of present interests in property currently is $15,000, and spouses can gift-split, thereby increasing the exemption amount to $30,000. Gifts given directly to colleges (for tuition, etc.) and health care providers for care are exempt. Also, a gift to a 529 plan can be equally split over five years for purposes of the annual exclusion. An unlimited exclusion exists for gifts to spouses and charities. Exempted and excluded gifts do not count at all towards the $11.4M limit.

Under Code section 1014, assets owned at death receive a "step up" in their adjusted basis to fair market value (or a step-down, if the assets have lost value). Assets in a revocable trust are deemed owned by the grantor upon death of the grantor. Assets held in an irrevocable trust are not subject to section 1014. So, estate planning involving an irrevocable trust that causes assets to be excluded from an individual's estate has lost much of its appeal.

"Portability" exists upon the death of the first spouse of any unused exemption amount (i.e. the $11.4M), such that the unused amount upon the first spouse's death can be used by the second spouse to die. Portability generally eliminates the (prior law) need to split the assets of estates of married persons. Even if an estate tax is not due, an estate tax return ordinarily must be filed for portability to apply.

At death, property generally passes in one of three ways—by will, death beneficiary designation or deed. Regardless how property transfers, it is included in a person's gross estate for estate tax purposes. Again, in 2019, hardly anyone pays estate or gift tax.

Tax Credits. Tax credits reduce the calculated tax. Some credits are refundable and other credits are nonrefundable. A refundable credit is one that can actually pay money to the taxpayer if tax liability is exceeded. A nonrefundable credit cannot result in payment to the taxpayer. It can only reduce tax liability.

Earned Income Tax Credit (or Earned Income Credit—"EITC" or "EIC") — The EITC is a refundable tax credit paid to persons whose income is relatively low. It is designed to increase cash for people who work. The credit is refundable, so it will be paid to the taxpayer if it exceeds the taxpayer's tax liability. The credit decreases as income increases. It increases with family size. The IRS provides online guidance concerning the credit, including Publication 596. There are private company-produced online calculators that calculate the credit, although some of them may not be accurate.

The Tax Policy Center estimated the 2015 cost of the EITC to be $69 billion.

Child Tax Credit — As amended by TCJA, the child tax credit for 2019 is $2,000 per child, with up to $1,400 of the tax credit being refundable. To be eligible, the child must not have attained age 17 during the year. Beginning in 2018, an addition credit of up to $500 is available for dependents other than minor children, if the dependent classification requirements are met. The ability to take the credit phases out for married persons filing jointly at a rate of $50 per $1,000 of modified AGI (or fraction thereof) in excess of $110,000. The same phase-out applies to single taxpayers once modified AGI hits $75,000. For almost all taxpayers, modified AGI equals AGI.

American Opportunity Tax Credit — This college costs credit reduces tax liability and, to a certain degree, provides cash payments if the credit exceeds tax liability. The credit is 100 percent of the first $2,000 of college expenses for each student, plus 25 percent of the next $2,000 of expenses. Up to 40 percent of the credit is refundable. The credit phases out as income increases. The credit phases out between $80,000 and $90,000 of modified adjusted gross income (typically equal to AGI) for single filers and $160,000 to $180,000 of MAGI for joint filers. The student must be enrolled at least half-time, and be working towards a degree, etc. For each child, four years of eligibility exist. However, the education expenses potentially subject to the credit are reduced by tax-free educational assistance received, including Pell grants. For purposes of both this credit and the Lifetime Learning Credit, amounts sourced from Section 529 plans are not eligible expenses.

Lifetime Learning Credit — This credit is available on an individual basis. The maximum credit for any year is $2,000. It does not vary by family size. The credit is 20 percent of the first $10,000 spent on qualified education at a qualified educational institution. As little as one course can be taken. Concerning years of eligibility, there is no limit. Eligibility for the credit phases out as income increases. For 2019, the phase-out occurs between $58,000 and $68,000 of MAGI for single filers and $116,000 to $136,000 of MAGI for married filing jointly taxpayers. The credit is coordinated with the American Opportunity Tax Credit, such that a taxpayer can elect to receive one or the other, but not both, in any given tax year.

Retirement Savings Contributions (Saver's) Tax Credit —The saver's tax credit is available for contributions to 401(k) plans, similar elective deferral plans and IRAs for certain persons. The annual credit is a percent of the amount contributed to an IRA or 401(k) plan, up to $2,000. The percent decreases as AGI increases. For 2019, for married persons filing jointly, the credit is 50 percent if AGI does not exceed $38,500, 20 percent for AGI between 38,500 and $41,500, and 10 percent for AGI above $41,500 but not in excess of $64,000. For single persons, the credit is 50 percent if AGI does not exceed $19,250, 20 percent if AGI is between $19,250 and $20,750, and 10 percent if AGI is greater than $20,750 but not more than $32,000.

Child and Dependent Care Credit — A tax credit is available for costs paid for childcare for children under age 13, if the childcare is necessary for the taxpayer (or spouse, if married and a joint return is filed) to be able to work or look for work. The maximum amount that is considered for the credit is $3,000 for one child and $6,000 for two or more children. The credit is nonrefundable. The credit percentage decreases as AGI increases. If AGI does not exceed $15,000, the credit percentage is 35. For taxpayers with AGI in excess of $15,000, the credit percent is decreased by one percentage point for each $2,000 or fraction thereof of AGI in excess of $15,000. However, the minimum credit percent is 20, and it applies to taxpayers with AGI in excess of $43,000. So, the minimum credit is $600 for one child and $1,200 for two or more children.

Obamacare (ACA) Credit — The formula for Obamacare premium tax credits is provided in Internal Revenue Code section 36B. These credits are refundable. They reduce the health care premium costs to an individual or household. The credit is based on the second lowest price for silver coverage in the geographic area where the individual or family resides.

Obamacare provides for platinum, gold, silver, and bronze coverage options, with the expected actuarial out-of-pocket costs to the insured increasing as the metal value decreases. As income increases, the credit amount decreases. The credit begins at 100 percent when income equals the Federal Poverty Level (FPL). The credit fully phases out at 400 percent of the FPL. Income is MAGI. (For most persons, MAGI is adjusted gross income (AGI).) According to a Bloomberg Businessweek article by Caroline Chen dated February 20, 2014 and titled, "Obamacare Consumers Avoiding Cheapest Health Plans," a U.S. Department of Human Services report stated that 62 percent of Obamacare enrollees had chosen mid-level silver plans. Thus, the premium credits have attracted consumers. As discussed in Chapter 6, prior to 2018, cost-sharing subsidies were available with respect to co-pays, co-insurance and deductibles for certain persons/households if silver coverage was elected.

In 2012, the U.S. Supreme Court ruled in *National Federation of Independent Businesses, et al. v. Sebelius* that Obamacare was constitutional. Part of Obamacare provides for expansion of Medicaid eligibility to persons and families with income not exceeding 138 percent of the FPL and effectively conditions receipt of federal Medicaid funds on expansion of eligibility. However, as part of the Supreme Court decision, the Court ruled that the states could decide whether to expand Medicaid coverage to persons and families with income not exceeding 138 percent of the FPL without losing federal funding for Medicaid. A majority of states have adopted Obamacare's expansion of Medicaid.

The individual mandate of Obamacare does not apply after 2018. Under the pre-2019 individual mandate, certain individuals were required to obtain a minimum level of coverage or be subjected to penalties.

Adoption Credit—A tax credit is available for adoption expenses. For 2019, the maximum credit is $14,080. As previously noted, if an employer provides adoption assistance benefits, up to $14,080 of benefits can be excluded. The ability to take tax credits or exclude income is phased out for modified AGI between $211,160 and $251,160 (so that no tax benefits are available if modified AGI exceeds $251,160.)

Miscellaneous Credits—Other credits exist, including one of up to $7,500 for purchasing an electric vehicle. A credit exists for lower income persons age 65 or greater, or who were retired due to total and permanent disability. TCJA added a tax credit for certain employers of up to 25 percent of pay made to non-highly paid employees on family and medical leave for up to 12 weeks per year. A 30 percent credit is available for purchase of property that uses solar energy to heat or cool a home, or to produce electricity for a home.

Planning

Once you understand the system, you can plan to minimize taxes. In the past, attorneys, CPAs and financial planners were generally called on to provide planning thoughts. And, a solid knowledge of the tax system and some commonly understood laws was often all that was necessary to provide effective planning. That's still the case for a segment of the population—for wealthy people. However, in recent years, tax planning needs to be done in light of entitlements, including federal financial aid for college. This is so because entitlements have been significantly expanded in recent years, such that even some upper middle income persons and households can garner some benefits. A tax-wise act might be imprudent from an entitlements standpoint. Entitlements are discussed in the Chapter 11.

Aside from expansion of entitlements, the financial problems of the U.S. and complexity of the tax system summarized in Chapter 1 need to be considered while planning. In the past, tax planners generally assumed that the current law (as provided for currently and into the future) would remain the law. However, given the nation's financial problems, using the current law to plan might be unreasonable. However, what can be used to plan other than the current law?

Federal Income Tax Planning. Over the years, gaps in the income tax system have led to legislative and regulatory patches to fill the gaps. There are very few gaps of significance or "loopholes," if any, left in the system. Nevertheless, there are things that can be done to reduce tax liability and/or increase entitlements.

The income tax system has a progressive rate structure, with individual tax rates ranging from 10 percent to 37 percent. If one knows his or her (or their) income is relatively high in the current year and will be much lower in the following year, and the system is not expected to significantly change over the next year, it would ordinarily be wise to accelerate deductions and defer income to the extent possible. For a cash method taxpayer (as defined above), these actions could include buying supplies near year-end and postponing billing near year-end. This strategy might also be employed if one's business is relatively constant, but a tax decrease is slated to take place in the following year. It is very likely that few changes will exist in 2020 other than those noted.

Example. It is November, and Joe's consulting practice has been very busy this year because of a law that is set to expire at year-end. Joe's income through the first nine months of the year is significantly greater than what he has experienced in most prior years. He expects next year's income to be much lower. His deductions have not changed much since prior years. Next year, the tax system is not expected to change much with respect to Joe. Joe sends out his bill every one to three months, depending on how busy he is at the given time. As Joe expects to be busy through year-end, waiting until January to send bills for work done in the last couple of months of the year would probably reduce Joe's combined liability for the current year and next year.

Example. Sue, who is self-employed, is having her best year in many years. She is doing so largely because of an industry development that will expire by year-end. She does not anticipate significant changes in the tax system relative to her in the upcoming year. She could pay her 4th quarter state estimated income tax installment, which is due on January 15th of 2020, in December of 2019. She could also pay her January rent in December. (Note: In the unlikely event Sue was subject to the alternative minimum tax (AMT), this strategy would not help with respect to state income tax because state income taxes are not deductible for AMT purposes. Also, TCJA greatly expanded the standard deduction, causing the percent of households that itemize to diminish substantially.)

TCJA significantly reduced the ability of some to deduct charitable contributions (due to the high standard deductions). For those who have a lot of itemized deductions and make significant charitable contributions, but not enough of reach the standard deduction limit, it might be prudent to "bunch up" on deductions every other year, so that a tax benefit is received.

Married persons can file their annual income tax return either jointly or separately. Generally, it is best for them to file jointly if one spouse has substantially more income than the other spouse (or if one spouse has no income). Tax software can be purchased to process a couple's taxes both ways. Some software used to produce the prior year's tax return can also be used to plan for the current year's taxes.

If a taxpayer has a small business that uses much equipment, buying a capital asset and "expensing" it for tax purposes can greatly reduce income. A capital asset is one that ordinarily must be "booked" as an asset and "written off" through depreciation deductions over two or more years because the asset is expected to have a useful life that extends beyond a year. In contrast, purchases that are immediately consumed or will be consumed (or used up) within a year can be immediately deducted (i.e. expensed). An example of a payment that can be expensed is a monthly rental payment. In contrast, a purchase of a building or a vehicle would ordinarily have to be capitalized.

Under Internal Revenue Code section 179, up to $1,020,000 of new or used business capital asset-type property can be expensed. Roofing, security systems, air conditioning and heating units used by a business potentially qualify. The amount that can be expensed is phased-out on a dollar-for-dollar basis once section 179 purchases exceed $2,550,000 for the year. In no event can the deduction produce a tax loss (and any loss that cannot be taken is carried forward). Under Code section 168(k), 100 percent of most depreciable new or used property other than real property generally can be expensed in the year of purchase. (This provision is coordinated with section 179.)

Self-employed persons can greatly reduce their tax liability by adopting a tax-qualified retirement plan or simplified employee pension (SEP). A tax-qualified plan can be adopted at any time before year-end. However, with respect to the 401(k) feature of a tax-qualified plan that is a profit sharing/401(k) plan, any deferral election of income must be made before income is payable to the self-employed person during the year. So, a 401(k) plan must be adopted before any elective deferrals can be made to it. In contrast, a profit sharing contribution can be made to the profit sharing component of a profit sharing/401(k) plan at any time prior to the due date of the taxpayer's tax return, including any extension of time to file. A SEP can be adopted up until the due date of the taxpayer's income tax return, including any extension of time to file. (All individuals are automatically entitled to a 6-month extension of time to file Form 1040, if they request the extension by April 15th.)

Up to 25 percent of compensation (or income, for a self-employed person) can be contributed to a SEP or the profit sharing component of a profit sharing/401(k) plan. For self-employed persons, the income is reduced by the deduction, thereby creating a circular equation that results in a net contribution limit of roughly 20 percent. However, for a profit sharing/401(k) plan, additionally, 401(k) elective deferrals (up to $19,000 in 2019) can be made that are not subject to the 25 percent limit. People age 50 or older can also make "catch-up" contributions (up to $6,000 in 2019). Thus, for providing deductible retirement contributions, a tax-qualified plan is a better mechanism than a SEP.

Reducing income, whether via tax-qualified plan contributions or otherwise, often opens up the availability of certain tax deductions and credits. Many deductions and credits "phase out" as income or AGI increases. Consequently, they phase back in as income or AGI decreases. For example, the Saver's credit is available to married persons filing jointly with AGI below $64,000 in 2019. (This credit is available to elective contributions.) Again, having tax software that permits one to estimate the current year's tax can be very helpful when trying to make tax-effective choices. As noted in Chapter 8, a cash balance pension plan can often provide an even better means of reducing income.

Example. The year is 2017, and the date is December 20th. Eve is a 60 year-old self-employed professional. She has a 401(k)/profit-sharing plan. Her husband, Adam, retired in 2017 at age 64. He earned $23,455 in 2017 before retiring. After his retirement, the couple acquired Obamacare coverage and received premium credits. Using tax software, assuming expected business income of $156,546 and other income of $25,517 for 2017, Eve realizes that unless she does something, she and Adam will owe approximately $55,000 in federal and state taxes. She calls her attorney/CPA on December 30th, inquiring about some options. A cash balance plan is considered. On December 31st, Eve makes a $24,000 contribution to her 401(k) profit-sharing plan and adopts a cash balance pension plan. The plan's formula is 10 percent of income up to $40,000 and 250 percent of income in excess of $40,000. The deduction range permits combined profit-sharing and cash balance contributions in the $80,000 range. Adopting and funding the plans by the due date of their return (plus extension, if applicable) reduces the federal and state tax liability to approximately $19,000. (Note: Real life example.)

Many can make a tax-deductible IRA contribution for a year, while also making a Roth IRA conversion for the year. If done in identical amounts, the result will ordinarily be a wash for tax purposes, but the taxpayer will have more IRA benefits and more Roth benefits.

Often, a tax liability is not known until after year-end. While a tax-qualified plan must be adopted by the end of the taxable year, a simplified employee pension (SEP), which essentially is an employer plan using IRAs, can be adopted up until (and contributions can be made up until) the due date of the taxpayer's income tax return, including any extension of time to file. Generally, up to 25 percent of each participant's compensation can be made to the SEP. Like a profit sharing plan contribution, a circular equation calculation applies to self-employed persons.

Because the maximum federal tax rate applicable to long-term capital gains is 20 percent while the maximum ordinary income tax rate is 37 percent, it is better for income to be capital gain than ordinary income. Planning can sometimes be done to convert what would be ordinary income into capital gain. For example, a sale of a number of lots of land would likely produce ordinary income because the seller is deemed to be in the business of selling land (and the land thus is inventory the sale of which produces ordinary income), whereas the seller of a single tract of land is more likely to be deemed to be an investor and the asset deemed to be a capital asset.

Generally, if an asset is sold and payment will take place over several years, the gain can be reported using the installment method of reporting. Under the installment method, the gain is prorated and "picked up" proportionately with receipt of the sales proceeds. For example, if a piece of land that cost $40,000 was sold for $100,000, with the payments to be made in five equal annual installments of $20,000 each, the $60,000 gain would be picked up in five $12,000 increments over five years. By spreading the income, overall tax is generally reduced because of the progressive nature of the income tax system.

Sometimes, a desire to accelerate income exists. In this regard, taxpayers can generally opt for the installment method not to apply. For example, a taxpayer might want to accelerate income in a year in which a large business loss or deduction (e.g. charitable) has been experienced or is anticipated to be experienced.

As previously noted, net capital losses are deductible up to $3,000. If a loss is taken on an asset sale (e.g. a stock sale) and the asset is repurchased within 30 days, the sale is considered to be a "wash sale," and the loss is disallowed. However, the repurchased asset will have a tax adjusted basis equal to its cost plus the loss that could not be taken.

Example. Joan has owned 100 shares of XYZ stock for five years. She bought the stock for $10,000. It is now worth $7,500. The value has not changed much for many months, and Joan does not expect the value of XYZ stock to change much for many months. Joan sells the stock for $7,500 on December 10, 2019. She buys 100 shares of XYZ stock on January 15, 2020 for $7,400. Joan can take a $2,500 long-term capital loss on her 2019 income tax return. If Joan had repurchased on January 5, 2020, she could not take a loss, and the adjusted basis of her XYZ shares would be $9,900 (i.e. $7,400 + $2,500).

Certain investments are tax-savvy. For example, interest income from investment in state and local government bonds generally is tax-exempt under the individual income tax system. However, depending on its nature, such interest may be taxable under the AMT.

As noted above, the passive activity loss (PAL) rules of Code section 469 can limit a taxpayer's ability to take a loss from a business investment. (A PAL can only be deducted against passive income, with unused losses carried forward. If not used, a PAL can be "taken" when the investment is sold, etc.) Similarly, the adjusted basis rules applicable to partnerships and S corporations can limit the amount of losses that can be taken in a year. Depending on the circumstances, it might be possible to do things to allow an anticipated loss to flow through to a taxpayer's return. For example, if the taxpayer works 450 hours for a non-real estate business, increasing the hours to 501 would satisfy the PAL rules (causing a loss not to be passive). Making a capital contribution to a partnership (or LLC) or an S corporation would create basis and thus possibly permit recognition of losses that would otherwise be suspended due to the loss limit rules. Of course, the tail should not wag the dog, and an investment should not be made if the cash detriment will outweigh the tax benefit (such as when the business is on shaky financial footing).

Numerous tax credits are summarized above, including the American Opportunity Tax Credit and the Lifetime Learning Credit. These credits relate to education, and they are coordinated so as to prevent "double dipping." While these credits generally apply for payments made during the year, up to three months of expenses for the following year can be paid in advance and qualify for one of the credits.

<u>Example</u>: Bob and Denise pay part of their child's college education expenses, and their income is low enough that they can take advantage of at least one of the credits. Late in 2019, Bob and Denise could prepay college expenses due for the first three months of 2020, and take either the American Opportunity Tax Credit or the Lifetime Learning Credit on their 2019 federal income tax return.

Life insurance investments produce tax-free income. Thus, if a policy is purchased for $10,000 and the insured dies the next month while the policy death benefit is $1,000,000, the entire $1,000,000 would be recovered free of income tax.

Gifts have no significance under the individual income tax system. The recipient takes an adjusted basis in the gift equal to the donor's basis, except that if the value at the time of the gift is less than the donor's basis, the value is the gift recipient's adjusted basis for purposes of computing loss. Assets passing at death receive a new adjusted basis—fair market value. Thus, if an elderly person wishes to gift some of his or her assets, it ordinarily is best to gift the assets that have either depreciated in value or have not experienced significant appreciation. Assets that have significantly appreciated are best left for pass at death, thereby receiving a "step up" in basis to fair market value.

Importantly, subject to limits previously noted, appreciated assets can be given to charity without income recognition. Thus, a stock that is worth $10,000 but cost the donor $1,000 would give rise to a $10,000 deduction. The $9,000 gain inherent in the stock would not be taxed.

Individuals age 70½ or older can cause their IRA assets of up to $100,000 to be transferred to a charity without recognition of income or a charitable deduction.

(The ordinary charitable deduction limits do not apply.) This tax provision if a good way for a senior to provide for charity while minimizing taxes, particularly if some or all of a minimum required distribution (generally applicable after the person has attained age 70½) is the source of the charitable contribution.

Numerous mechanisms exist to provide charitable deductions to charities while allowing the donor or his or her beneficiaries to continue to reap some benefit from the assets given—either over the near term or at some point in the future. Charitable remainder "unitrusts" (CRUTs), charitable remainder annuities (CRATs) and pooled income funds (PIFs) all permit a current income tax deduction for contribution of a remainder interest (i.e. an interest in property payable in the future) to a charity. The income of the trust is payable to a person or persons until an event, such as death. Thereafter, the assets are given to the charity. The present value of the future interest given to the charity is currently deductible for income tax purposes. Oppositely, a charitable lead trust grants the charity an income interest for a term of years, followed by transfer of the property to a person or persons. The present value of the "lead" interest produces a deduction.

For those who own a business and want a deduction without a cash outlay, a grant of an equity interest therein to an employee would ordinarily result in a compensation deduction for the value of the equity interest provided. However, having an employee as an equity interest holder can create problems. For example, if the company is an S corporation, a transfer of the stock by the employee to an ineligible shareholder would "blow" the S election. Accordingly, care should be undertaken through a shareholders' agreement (for a corporation) or an operating agreement (for an LLC) to prevent undesirable action by any equity interest holder.

As explained in Chapter 8, there are two types of IRAs: traditional and Roth. A traditional IRA is generally created either by tax-deductible contributions to the traditional IRA custodian or via transfer ("rollover") of assets from a tax-qualified plan to a traditional IRA. A Roth IRA is an IRA ordinarily created by non-deductible contributions to the Roth IRA, conversion of a traditional IRA to a Roth IRA or rollover of Roth funds from a tax-qualified plan (ordinarily, a 401(k) plan). Generally and very importantly, if amounts are distributed from a Roth IRA, they are first sourced from "basis" (i.e. amounts that were converted or Roth IRA contributions), and thereafter are sourced from earnings.

For those who believe the income tax system will continue in its current form or something close to it indefinitely, Roth IRA conversions and, where available through a 401(k) plan, Roth 401(k) contributions, should be considered in years when income is anticipated to be relatively low. For example, a medical intern making little money currently but expecting to make a lot of money in the future might make a Roth 401(k) contribution (or conversion) that costs her little because she is in a relatively low income tax bracket. The assets will grow tax-free, and would ordinarily be received tax-free in retirement. As noted in Chapter 1, the financial problems of the federal government make indefinite tax-free Roth benefits less than certain. More Roth options are discussed in Chapter 8, Saving for Retirement.

Example: Elaine is a medical intern studying to be a neurosurgeon. Currently, she makes $30,000 per year. She is single, and she feels confident that her federal/state incremental income tax bracket will be 15 percent or less.

Virtually every graduate of her program makes over $200,000 per year in the year following graduation, and income only increases thereafter. Elaine could make a $6,000 contribution to a Roth IRA, thus creating a tax-free account that should produce tax-free income in the future. (A traditional IRA contribution would have only saved $900 of taxes if a 15 percent combined federal/state rate applies.) Also, if Elaine has a traditional IRA, she could elect to convert all or part of it to a Roth IRA, pay a low federal tax (and perhaps state income tax), and then have an account that should produce tax-free income in the future.

Example: Ken is the sole owner of an S corporation. The corporation, which is Ken's sole income source, ordinarily produces $50,000 to $100,000 of taxable income. However, due to a lawsuit settlement that cost the company $100,000, the company has a net loss of $20,000 for 2019. Ken owns a $25,000 traditional IRA. Ken is married and he and his wife file a joint return. His wife makes $10,000 to $20,000 each year from working part-time. Ken determines that he and his wife will pay no federal income taxes for 2019, and they could have up to an additional $12,000 of income without becoming subject to income tax. Ken converts $12,000 of his traditional IRA to a Roth IRA on December 15, 2019. The conversion costs $0, and the future Roth benefits should be tax-free.

For the owner(s) of a business that wish to sell their business to their employees, an employee stock ownership plan (ESOP) provides tremendous tax advantages. If the corporation is a C corporation and at least 30 percent of the stock is owned by the ESOP following a sale to the ESOP, any gain is tax-free as long as the selling shareholder purchases certain traditional stocks and bonds of a certain nature as a replacement investment. (The selling shareholder takes a basis in the stocks and bonds equal to the basis previously held in the corporation's stock.) After the sale, the corporation could make an S election, thereby causing income received by the ESOP to be tax-free. (The corporation would pay no tax on its income, because it is an S corporation.) If all of the stock of the company was sold to the ESOP, all of the net income of the company (allocated to the ESOP after the sale and the S election) would be tax-free income.

Finally, as noted, it is possible to purchase tax software that allows one to prepare the prior year's return and do tax planning for the current year. Planning devices for the current year cannot be entirely accurate (and therefore cannot be entirely relied on) because Congress often passes laws late in the year that extend existing tax provisions or makes new laws. However, if the tax system is not expected to change substantially (as generally is the case), particularly for self-employed persons, planning close to year-end (i.e. in the latter half of December) can often produce substantial tax and entitlements benefits.

Federal Estate and Gift Tax Planning. As this book is aimed at people and households making $75,000 to $400,000 per year and the combined estate and lifetime gift tax exemption is $11.4 million in 2019, presumably no one reading this book will have estate or gift tax concerns. A 40 percent tax rate applies to amounts in excess of the exemption amount.

The estate and gift tax system taxes wealth that an individual transfers during life or following death in excess of $11.4 million (in 2019—the amount is annually indexed for inflation). Gifts and amounts passing at death have no estate or gift tax consequences until the $11.4 million threshold has been surpassed. Consequently, less than 0.1 percent of the U.S. population is now subject to the estate and gift tax. A separate generation-skipping tax (GST), with the same exemption, generally applies to any bequest (direct or through a trust) that "skips" a generation (i.e. is made to grandchildren or more distant heirs, rather than to children). Certain gifts and bequests are exempted from the analysis.

The annual exclusion for gifts of present interests in property is $15,000 in 2019, and spouses can gift-split, thereby increasing the exemption amount to $30,000. Gifts given directly to colleges (for tuition, etc.) and health care providers for care are exempt. Gifts to 529 plans for college savings can be treated as deemed made in five equal installments for purposes of the annual exclusion. Unlimited gifts can be made to spouses and charities. These excluded and exempted gifts and bequests do not count *at all* towards the $11.4 million limit.

Sometimes, for reasons discussed in Chapter 3, assets are transferred to a revocable trust for estate planning purposes. Assets in a revocable trust are deemed owned by the grantor (i.e. the creator of the trust) upon death of the grantor for estate tax purposes. Under Code section 1014, assets owned at death receive a "step up" in tax adjusted basis to fair market value (or a step-down, if the assets have depreciated). Since adjusted basis of an asset is used to calculate gain or loss on sale, an increase in adjusted basis is helpful. Therefore, as previously explained, it is generally advisable for a person near death to retain substantially appreciated assets so their value can be "stepped up" at death. If a desire to gift exist, it would be best to gift assets with a relatively higher adjusted basis (relative to value). Thus, the appeal of trusts that cause assets to be excluded from an individual's estate (e.g. through a trust that is not a grantor trust) has lost much of its appeal.

Example: Sally is old and wealthy. She wishes to transfer all of her wealth to her two children. She owns two substantial assets—stock in X company worth $3,000,000 that has an adjusted basis of $1,000,000 and stock in Y company worth $3,000,000 that has an adjusted basis of $2,900,000. The stock of both X company and Y company is publicly-traded, and Sally has no reason to think the values are anything other than their publicly-traded values. Sally wishes to transfer a total of $3,000,000 of wealth to her children, in equal shares, immediately. If Sally transfers the Y company stock, her children will have an adjusted basis in their shares equal to her basis of $2,900,000. A sale by the children would produce only $100,000 of combined gain. If instead, she transferred the X company stock, a sale by the children would produce a total gain of $2,000,000. By keeping the X company stock, its adjusted basis will be stepped up at her death to fair market value (a $2,000,000 adjustment at the time analyzed above). So, it would be best to gift the Y company stock.

Sometimes, it is beneficial to make a completed gift for estate and gift tax purposes, but for the taxable income of the trust to be taxed to the grantor (so as to reduce income taxes). An "intentionally defective grantor trust" is sometimes used for this purpose. Such a trust provides a complete and irrevocable gift for estate and gift tax purposes (thus taking the property out of the grantor's estate) while causing the grantor to be taxed on the trust's annual net income. Generally, an intentionally defective grantor trust is an irrevocable grantor trust from which the grantor cannot benefit.

"Portability" exists upon the death of the first spouse of any unused exemption amount (i.e. the $11.4 million), such that the unused amount upon the first spouse's death can be used by the second spouse to die. Portability generally eliminates the need to split estates to avoid wasting exemptions. Even if an estate tax is not due, an estate tax return ordinarily must be filed for portability to apply. If you are wealthy enough to be potentially subject to estate tax (or gift tax), you should seek counseling regarding the matter.

Example: Sam and Patty have been married for many years. They have accumulated $18,000,000 of wealth. Of the total, $14,000,000 is owned by Sam, mainly through tax-qualified plans and IRAs. The wills of Sam and Patty provide that all of the assets owned will pass to the survivor of the two of them upon death, and the assets will pass to their descendants with respect to the second to die. The wills also provide for a disclaimer, whereby assets disclaimed by the surviving spouse will pass immediately to descendants. If Sam dies (first), the assets passing to Patty will qualify for the marital deduction. Sam's unused $11.4 million exemption can be fully used by Patty's estate following her death. When she later dies, assuming she has not made prior gifts than exceeded the annual exclusion, the sum of whatever the exemption amount is in the year of her death plus $11.4 million will not be subject to the estate tax. If Patty had disclaimed $3 million of the bequest to her, such that only $11 million passed to her, $3 million of Sam's exemption would be applied by his estate following his death, leaving only $8.4 million of exemption to pass to Patty (i.e. $11.4 million minus $3 million).

For those with significant life insurance and the possibility that an estate tax could be payable, it might be wise to establish and fund an irrevocable life insurance trust ("ILIT"). If established so that the insured grantor cannot change beneficiaries or access the life insurance policy, etc., then the policy proceeds are excluded from the grantor's estate. Generally, if an existing policy is transferred to an ILIT, the grantor insured must survive for at least three years in order for the policy benefits to be excluded from the grantor's estate.

Chapter 6

Benefiting from Obamacare

Given the very uncertain nature of health care in the U.S., what is provided below could have changed by the time you read this material. The author believes it is accurate as of January 1, 2019. So, please keep this reality in mind as you read these materials. However, the author believes it is highly unlikely that Obamacare will change substantially in 2019. In this regard, Congress ordinarily gives people reasonable time to act when something beyond their control can potentially substantially detrimentally impact them.

Many people assume that the benefits of the Affordable Care Act ("ACA" or Obamacare) are available only to lower and middle income households. The reality is, ACA benefits can extend to upper middle income households, and the benefits can be substantial.

The ACA created four general metal categories of coverage, with the actuarial value of coverage decreasing as the value of the metal decreases. The metals and their actuarial values are platinum (90 percent), gold (80 percent), silver (70 percent) and bronze (60 percent).

Premium tax credits are available to households with income equal to or exceeding 100 percent but not exceeding 400 percent of the federal poverty level (FPL). For 2019, for a family of four, the FPL is $25,750. Four-hundred percent of the FPL is $100,400. It is very important to note two things: (1) "income" means modified adjusted gross income (MAGI), which for most households means Adjusted Gross Income (AGI); and (2) *accumulated wealth is irrelevant*. So, a family of four with gross income of $125,000, AGI of

$70,000 and $5,000,000 of accumulated net worth could qualify for substantial benefits.

Monthly premium tax credits decrease as MAGI rises above 100 percent of the FPL. At exactly 100 percent of the FPL, the average premium tax credit for a four-person family is $2,217. At 200 percent, the amount is $1,987. At 300 percent, it is $1,642. At 398 percent, it is $1,439. At 400.1 percent, it is $0.

Generally speaking, Obamacare must be "signed up for" before the beginning of a calendar year. Exceptions exist. Enrollment for a year begins on the preceding November 1st.

One of the main criticisms of Obamacare is that it has forced coverage of many unhealthy persons, thus driving up health insurance premiums for all. For persons who must buy coverage but cannot take advantage of the premium subsidies, the cost of coverage is much greater than it would have been without Obamacare. But, more people are covered.

In addition to premium credits, as enacted, the ACA provided for substantial cost sharing subsidies (i.e. reduced deductibles, co-insurance and co-pays) to households with MAGI equal to or exceeding 100 percent but not exceeding 250 percent of the FPL, as long as "silver" coverage was elected. The cost-sharing subsidies benefits decreased for income in excess of 150 percent of the FPL, and then again for income in excess of 200 percent of the FPL. Again, there were no net worth limitations.

According to a December 27, 2018 *healthinsurance.org* article by Louise Norris, the Trump Administration stopped funding cost sharing subsidies in the fall of 2017. Insurers kept what the insured have to pay out-of-pocket for deductibles and co-pays constant, and added the cost (of covering part or all of deductibles and co-pays) to the premiums, thus making silver coverage disproportionately expensive. Since the ACA establishes premium credits by setting the maximum people must pay, and premium credits are based on a benchmark silver plan, the net effect has been increased premium credits for silver coverage. Ms. Norris noted: "This continues to be the case in 2019, and disproportionately large premium subsidies are even more widespread for 2019 than they were for 2018." The article then notes that because such subsidies are so large, some enrollees can get bronze coverage for free, or gold coverage for less than the cost of silver coverage.

It should be noted that in many states that have not expanded Medicaid in the way anticipated by Obamacare, there is a "coverage gap." Thus, people who have lower income (below 100 percent of the FPL), but income that is too high to qualify for Medicaid, may be ineligible for ACA benefits. Such persons may be able to purchase catastrophic coverage. For states that expanded Medicaid to cover income up to 138 percent of the FLP, eligibility for ACA benefits begins when income is 139 percent of the FPL.

To be eligible for the forgoing benefits, health coverage *must* be purchased on the ACA health care exchange. To be eligible to purchase health care on the ACA exchange and potentially qualify for ACA benefits, a person must not be eligible for certain other coverage, including Medicare, Medicaid, CHIP, Tricare or affordable minimum essential coverage from an employer. Affordable generally means the cost does not exceed 9.5 percent of family income. Minimum essential coverage means bronze coverage or better, in terms of costs covered by the plan. So, self-employed persons and owners of small businesses may qualify. If affordable minimum essential coverage is not provided then, depending on how many employees exist, penalties can potentially apply to the employer.

Consider the benefits for the following four person family using the projected 2019 tax system. One person age 50+ works and makes $100,000. In scenario 1, the family purchases a high deductible health plan (HDHP) outside an ACA exchange for $1,337/month, does not contribute to any retirement plans or IRAs, and also does not contribute to an HSA. In scenario 2, HDHP coverage is purchased for $1,337/month outside an exchange, and deductible contributions of $45,000 are made to retirement plans for the self-employed person, $7,000 to an HSA and $6,000 to the spouse's IRA. Scenario 3 is the same as Scenario 2, except the health care coverage is purchased through an ACA exchange at a gross cost of $1,337/month. Scenario 4 is the same as Scenario 3, except silver coverage is purchased for a gross cost of $1,880/month through the ACA exchange and no HSA contribution is made. Considering only federal taxes, the net cash flows follow. Note: Deductibles and co-pays are less under scenario 4 than they are under the other three scenarios.

Obamacare Analysis 2019

Scenario:	1	2	3	4
Business Income	100,000	100,000	100,000	100,000
20% QBI Deduction	13,707	2,107	2,107	2,107
Modified AGI	92,935	34,935	34,935	34,935
Federal Tax (A)	17,821	12,370	(3,314)	(7,627)
Health Insurance (B)	16,044	16,044	16,044	22,560
Net Tax and Health Care (A + B)	33,865	28,414	12,730	14,933

State tax savings only increase the differences. If Georgia law applied, an additional $3,480 of savings would exist under Scenario 3 compared to Scenario 1. Including Georgia state tax, the total difference between Scenarios 1 and 3 is $24,615.

If income rose *by $50,000* to $150,000 under scenario 3, the family's MAGI would be $82,030. This figure is well below 400 percent of the FPL for the family in 2019 (i.e. $103,000), meaning the family could still claim a substantial premium tax credit under the ACA.

Planning Hypothetical: Given the four scenarios listed above and assuming Georgia is the state of residence, and further assuming the taxpayer and his spouse have $160,000 in Roth IRAs with a $100,000 basis, is it best to use $58,000 of Roth IRA assets to fund the retirement and HSA benefits under Scenario 3 or pay the higher taxes and health care costs under Scenario 1?

The cash rate of savings on the retirement/HSA benefits is:
    (24,615/58,000) =   42 percent

Considerations: Including the HSA money as retirement money, there is no difference in retirement money. The Roth benefits would decrease by $58,000 (i.e. 45,000 + 7,000 + 6,000) and the pre-tax retirement and HSA benefits would increase by $58,000. However, the HSA funds should come out tax-free, leaving $51,000 of taxable benefits (i.e. 58,000 – 7,000). Thus, the retirement tax rate on all of the pre-tax money would need to be 48 percent (24,615/51,000) in order for the transaction to be a break-even transaction. (Below 48 percent, using the Roth money makes sense.) As the highest tax bracket in 2019 is 37 percent, it seems very unlikely such a rate would apply. But, consider the factors noted in Chapter 1, including the previous rates during World War II and in the 1950s. The couple would still have $102,000 of Roth benefits, which should be enough to provide significant tax leverage in retirement. Note: Federal financial aid for college is not considered to be relevant in the foregoing analysis. If it was relevant, the analysis would be different. *(End Hypothetical)*

Since ACA benefits decrease as MAGI increases, all other things equal, MAGI should be minimized to maximize ACA benefits while simultaneously reducing taxes. (However, MAGI needs to equal or exceed the FPL for premium credits, etc. to be available.) As noted in Scenarios 1-4, the retirement and HSA contributions reduced the QBI deduction. But, as explained in Chapter 8, the reduced QBI's value is greatly exceeded by the deductions' value. Certain things can be done to increase cash flow without increasing or substantially increasing MAGI. For example, Roth IRA distributions are tax-free to the extent of the sum of contributions and prior income recognition amounts relating to conversions. Also, if not needed for education, a distribution from a 529 account produces income only to the extent of the income earned (and income is recognized pro rata with basis when distributions are made). A 10 percent penalty also potentially applies to the income.

In addition to ACA benefits, a diminished AGI can make other tax benefits available. For example, for 2019, the Saver's Credit is generally available to married persons filing jointly with AGI below $64,000 and for single persons with AGI below $32,000. In scenario 3 above, for example, the Saver's credit saved an additional $843. It is important to note that a Roth distribution is income for purposes of FAFSA (i.e. college aid) purposes. So, even though a Roth distribution would ordinarily not be included in AGI (thus not reducing ACA benefits), it ordinarily would reduce FAFSA potential benefits.

For self-employed persons, very often, year-end planning can be done to substantially reduce taxes and increase ACA benefits. Many tax software packages include a tax planning option, whereby numbers can be used to project tax for the current year. Analyzing one's situation in mid-December can be a very prudent/beneficial action. Of the three deductions listed above, only 401(k) elective deferrals need be made before year-end. IRA and HSA contributions must be made by April 15th of the following year. If an extension is filed for the federal 1040 return, the profit sharing contribution can be made by as late as October 15th of the following year. If an S corporation exists, the due date and the extended due date would be a month earlier.

Other ACA benefits are available to small businesses, including tax credits to pay a substantial part of health care costs for up to two years. Certain small businesses are entitled to a 50 percent tax credit for two years with respect to payment of health care coverage for employees. To be eligible for the credit, the compensation of the employees must fall below a certain threshold. A deduction is available to the extent a credit is not taken.

The 21st Century Cures Act, enacted in late 2016, allows for stand-alone health reimbursement arrangements by small employers. These arrangements can only be offered by small employers—generally those with less than 50 full-time employees. No other plan can be offered by the employer. The program must be provided on the same terms to all employees, and it must be solely funded by the employer. The program must be limited to qualifying health expenses described in IRC section 213(d), and only employees and family members can participate. For 2019, benefits per year cannot exceed $5,150 for single employees and $10,450 per year for families. The following employees can be excluded from coverage: (i) part-time and seasonal employees; (ii) new hires with less than 90 days of employment; (iii) employees younger than age 25; (iv) union employees; and (v) nonresident aliens. Notice of the benefit program must ordinarily be provided at least 90 days before the beginning of the year. The amount of the benefits provided must be noted in W-2s. These programs are exempt from COBRA and most of ERISA. However, benefits reduce ACA premium credits.

Depending on the facts, it might be possible for one or more business owners to cover employees but not themselves under a business health plan, and then cover themselves and possibly their dependents under an individual policy or policies purchased on an ACA exchange. The individual policy could possibly qualify for the individual premium credit and cost sharing subsidies of the ACA.

Many people "freak out" when they hear the word *Obamacare*. Perhaps it is due to political reasons. However, as far a health care coverage, policies purchased through an ACA exchange are hard to distinguish from those purchased outside an ACA exchange. Given waivers granted by the Centers for Medicare and Medicaid Services since ACA enactment, Obamacare coverage should always be at least as comprehensive as other health insurance with equal deductibles and co-pays.

Exactly what type coverage should be obtained through Obamacare depends on the particular situation of the person or family acquiring coverage. People who will experience little health care needs and people who will experience tremendous health care needs (and costs) will ordinarily fare better under a high deductible health plan with an HSA. However, one should "run the numbers," based on anticipated needs, to determine what will likely be the best product.

While ACA tax benefits of maintaining a health can be substantial for small businesses, in many cases it will be best not to maintain a health plan and instead to pay the employees a little more in cash and let them apply for ACA benefits.

Example: Dave is the sole member of an LLC that runs a small business in Georgia. The business has three employees, A, B and C. A, who is married and age 50, has two young children and household income of $60,000. All of A's household income comes from the LLC. A defers $10,000 per year to the LLC's 401(k) plan. B is married and does not have children. B's household income is $65,000, of which $45,000 is earned by B from the LLC and the remainder is earned by B's spouse. B contributes $4,000 per year to the LLC's 401(k) plan. Like A, B's spouse is not eligible to participate in an employer-sponsored health plan. C is single and has household income of $45,000, all of which is earned by working for the LLC. (Dave knows their personal situations.) Dave's combined federal and state tax incremental bracket is 38 percent. Assume: (a) the annual health care premium costs for A's family would be $15,000; (b) the annual health care premium costs for B and his spouse would be $12,000; and (c) the annual health care premium cost for C would be $7,000. The total cost would be $34,000. Dave is considering sponsoring a health plan and reducing the employees' combined pay by $6,800 to cover 20 percent of the cost. Potential tax credits aside, doing so would annually cost Dave $16,344 (i.e. ((34,000-6,800) x (1 - .38)) – (6,800 x .0765)). If, instead, Dave paid the employees ten percent more in compensation (i.e. $6,000 for A, $4,500 for B and $4,500 for C, for a total of $15,000), his after-tax cost would be $10,447.50 (i.e. (15,000 x (1 - .38)) + (15,000 x .0765))). The employees could buy health coverage on the ACA exchange, and they would potentially be entitled to substantial ACA benefits that could reduce their health care costs tremendously. Depending on the individual facts of A, B and C, the net costs to them could be much less than the net costs that would have existed had Dave's LLC provided coverage. For example, if A lived in zip code 30126 and purchased bronze coverage under the pay increase scenario, the net excess of increased compensation over increased taxes and health care costs for A's family would be $6,925. (*End*)

ACA credits are calculated through one's tax return for the year. However, advance premium credits can be applied for to reduce health insurance premium costs during the year. It is generally advantageous to apply for advance premium credits, as there is a limit on the amount of an excess advance credit that must be repaid in the event the actual credit calculated with the tax return is less than the advanced premium credits. The maximum amount that must be repaid varies with income level. For 2018, for households with income less than 200 percent of the FPL, the maximum was $300 for single persons and $600 for couples and families. For those with income of 200 percent of the FPL or greater but less than 300 percent of the FPL, the amounts were $775 for single persons and $1,550 for couples and families. For income of 300 percent or greater but less than 400 percent of the FPL, the maximum repayment figures were $1,300 and $2,600 for single persons and couples/households, respectively. These amounts are annually indexed for inflation.

Ordinarily, ACA coverage must be chosen before a calendar year, and it cannot be changed mid-year. However, if a person's financial situation changes for the worse mid-year, due to various circumstances, it may be possible to have coverage (and advance premium credits) adjusted mid-year.

If an individual has the option of making HSA contributions or 401(k) contributions, but does not have enough funds to maximize both, which should be funded? It will ordinarily be prudent to maximize 401(k) contributions until matching contributions are maximized, and then fund HSA contributions to the maximum amount deductible. If the choice is between making an HSA contribution or an IRA contribution, it will generally be best to make an HSA contribution, as both are tax-deductible but HSA benefits ordinarily will be tax-free (while IRA benefits will be taxable).

HSA investments ordinarily can be invested in any investments made available by the HSA trustee or custodian. Often, the options are similar to those of a 401(k) plan. Particularly if a large balance does not exist, it may be best to invest HSA funds in cash, so as to prevent the need for liquidation, etc. in the event of a health care need. In this regard, other retirement funds should be viewed in tandem with HSA assets. HSA "shopping around" can pay off significantly.

Notes: The following assumptions apply in the four Scenarios listed above: The year is 2019. Net taxable income from self-employment is $100,000. Husband is age 50; wife is age 49. The kids are ages 8 and 10. The maximum DC retirement plan contribution (401(k)/profit sharing) is $45,000. A $6,000 IRA contribution was made by the spouse. The HSA contribution was $7,000. The silver coverage figures are based on the national average. Because there is no HSA contribution for silver coverage, MAGI is higher under scenario 4 than it is under scenario 3, resulting in lower premium tax credits.

Chapter 7

Federal Financial Aid for College

Most colleges and universities determine financial need using the Free Application for Federal Student Aid (FAFSA). ***Some colleges, particularly private ones, use a different analysis***. The FAFSA must be completed and filed to determine the Expected Family Contribution (EFC). The EFC is the minimum amount the family or student must pay towards college. The balance is paid for by government grants (including the Pell grant), institutional grants, private grants, work-study compensation and loans. Grants and loans are large sources of financial aid.

At some colleges, only the EFC must be paid. Colleges determine costs. Ordinarily, minimizing the EFC minimizes family/student potential costs.

For a family situation where the child is dependent, net worth and earnings of the parents and the child determine the EFC. For each schoolyear, the main source of FAFSA information is the parent's or parents' federal income tax return for the second year preceding the school year. So, for the 2019-2020 schoolyear FAFSA, the 2017 tax return is analyzed.

Generally, for the applicable year (2017, for the 2019-2020 school year), two separate calculations are added together to produce the EFC. A parents' calculation is done, and it is then added to the child's calculation.

The parents' (or parent's) calculation is done by (a) taking their adjusted gross income for the applicable year, (b) adjusting AGI by making several additions and subtractions, (c) adding a portion of 12 percent of the parents' net worth, (d) multiplying the total by a progressive factor (with the highest and probably most common being .47) and then (e) *dividing by the number of children in college,* to produce the parents' portion of the EFC.

A similar calculation is done for the child, except 20 percent of net worth is taken into account and there is no division for the number of children in college. A significant exemption allowance ($6,660) exists for income, meaning the addition to EFC for a child will generally be $0 if the child has no assets. The 2019-2020 dependent child form (with its two separate parts) is produced below.

One of the adjustments to adjusted gross income to produce EFC is addition of "untaxed income and benefits." The applicable statute (20 U.S.C. §1087vv) defines untaxed income and benefits rather generally. It includes child support, workman's compensation, veteran's benefits, tax-exempt interest, cash support paid on the student's behalf, untaxed pension benefits, payments to IRAs and Keogh accounts excluded from income and "any other untaxed income and benefits." While statutory authority exists for many of these things to be defined, there is very little regulatory guidance. Instead, guidance comes mainly from the instructions to the FAFSA form, some letters written by Department of Education officials and various articles. So, there is much that is grey.

Via the instructions to the FAFSA form, untaxable income includes 401(k) and IRA contributions for the return year. Self-employed persons must also add profit sharing contributions for the return year. These contributions must be added back because they are discretionary in nature. In contrast, a nondiscretionary contribution, such as a fixed one required to fund a pension plan of a company that employs the person, very likely would not be added back. (In this regard, as in many areas, FAFSA guidance is not entirely clear.) Income generally includes distributions from a Roth IRA or Roth 401(k) account.

There are three different FAFSA application forms: one for a dependent student; one for an independent student without dependents except a spouse; and one for an independent student with a dependent other than a spouse. With respect to the three options, who owns assets and who earns income can have a substantial impact on the financial outcome. Various means exist to determine if a student is independent. For the 2019-2020 school year, included in the group of independent students are: (a) students born before 1996; (b) married students; (c) students enrolled in a master's or doctoral degree program; (d) veterans; and (e) students who provide more than half of the support for a child of theirs. Numerous other possibilities exist.

Investments include cash, CDs, stocks, bonds, net equity in real estate, and Section 529 plan assets. *The home is exempt, as are all retirement savings.* As discussed below, the value of an interest in a small business is also exempt. A dollar amount exemption applies to investments. The exemption amount depends on whether there are one or two parents and the age of the oldest parent (for a one-parent family, the age of the parent). For example, if the oldest parent of a two-parent family with a dependent child student will be age 54 on December 31, 2019, the 2019 investment exemption amount is $13,900. Generally, debts reduce assets only to the extent they are secured by the asset.

The FAFSA for 2019-2020 may be filed on or after October 1, 2018. The deadline for submission will vary by school. Technically, the FAFSA deadline for the 2019-2020 school year is June 30, 2020. However, schools' earlier deadlines generally need to be met to receive school and/or state aid.) The applicant's net worth at the time of submission is what is pertinent to the EFC formula.

The best way to minimize the EFC is to minimize income for the four year period beginning with the calendar year the child will enter his or her junior year of high school, while minimizing assets owned at the time each application is submitted. So, if a child will begin college in 2021, minimizing income beginning in 2019 can help reduce cost.

With respect to the 2019-2020 school year, for dependent students from households where the income of the parent(s) was $26,000 or less in 2017, and where (a) certain low-income entitlements were received in 2017 or 2018, (b) there was no income tax filing requirement or Form 1040A or 1040EZ was filed, or (c) a parent of the household is a dislocated worker, the EFC is $0. The low-income entitlements include Medicaid, Supplemental Security Income (SSI), Supplemental Nutrition Assistance Program (SNAP), Free and Reduced Price School Lunch Program, Temporary Assistance for Needy Families (TANF) and the Special Supplemental Nutrition Program for Woman, Infants, and Children (WIC).

For the 2019-2020 schoolyear, if eligible for one or more of the low-income entitlements listed in the preceding paragraph and 2017 AGI was less than $50,000, assets are not considered in the EFC calculation. *Note: Carefully read the instructions to the FAFSA.* For some, online research will be necessary to determine the meanings of terms used on the form.

The 2019–2020 EFC formula for a full-time (i.e. enrolled at least nine months) dependent student follows. Note that it is in two pages. The first page relates to the parent(s). The second page primarily relates to the student.

PARENTS' INCOME IN 2017	
1. Parents' adjusted gross income (FAFSA/SAR #85) If negative, enter zero.	
2. a. Parent 1 (father/mother/stepparent) income earned from work (FAFSA/ SAR #88)	
2. b. Parent 2 (father/mother/stepparent) income earned from work (FAFSA/ SAR #89) +	
Total parents' income earned from work =	
3. Taxable income (If tax filers, enter the amount from line 1 above. If non-tax filers, enter the amount from line 2.)*	
4. Total untaxed income and benefits: (total of FAFSA/SAR #94a through 94i) +	
5. Taxable and untaxed income (sum of line 3 and line 4) =	
6. Total additional financial information (total of FAFSA/SAR #93a through 93f) –	
7. TOTAL INCOME (line 5 minus line 6) May be a negative number. =	

ALLOWANCES AGAINST PARENTS' INCOME	
8. 2017 U.S. income tax paid (FAFSA/SAR #86) (tax filers only) If negative, enter zero.	
9. State and other tax allowance (Table A1) If negative, enter zero. +	
10. Parent 1 (father/mother/stepparent) Social Security tax allowance (Table A2) +	
11. Parent 2 (father/mother/stepparent) Social Security tax allowance (Table A2) +	
12. Income protection allowance (Table A3) +	
13. Employment expense allowance: • Two working parents (Parents' Marital Status is "married" or "unmarried and both parents living together"): 35% of the lesser of the earned incomes, or $4,000, whichever is less • One-parent families: 35% of earned income, or $4,000, whichever is less • Two-parent families, one working parent: enter zero +	
14. TOTAL ALLOWANCES =	

*STOP HERE (at line 3) if the following are true:

Line 3 is $26,000 or less **and**

• The parents are eligible to file a 2017 IRS Form 1040A or 1040EZ (that is, they are not required to file a 2017 Form 1040) or they are not required to file any income tax return **or**

• Anyone included in the parents' household size (as defined on the FAFSA) received benefits during 2017 or 2018 from any of the designated means-tested federal benefit programs **or**

• Either of the parents is a dislocated worker.

If these circumstances are true, the Expected Family Contribution is automatically zero.

AVAILABLE INCOME	
TOTAL INCOME (from line 7)	
TOTAL ALLOWANCES (from line 14) –	
15. AVAILABLE INCOME (AI) May be a negative number. =	

PARENTS' CONTRIBUTION FROM ASSETS	
16. Cash, savings, and checking (FAFSA/SAR #90)	
17. Net worth of investments** (FAFSA/SAR #91) If negative, enter zero. +	
18. Net worth of business and/or investment farm (FAFSA/SAR #92) + If negative, enter zero.	
19. Adjusted net worth of business/farm (Calculate using Table A4.) +	
20. Net worth (sum of lines 16, 17, and 19) =	
21. Education savings and asset protection allowance (Table A5) –	
22. Discretionary net worth (line 20 minus line 21) =	
23. Asset conversion rate × .12	
24. CONTRIBUTION FROM ASSETS If negative, enter zero. =	

PARENTS' CONTRIBUTION	
AVAILABLE INCOME (AI) (from line 15)	
CONTRIBUTION FROM ASSETS (from line 24) +	
25. Adjusted available income (AAI) May be a negative number. =	
26. Total parents' contribution from AAI (Calculate using Table A6.) If negative, enter zero.	
27. Number in college in 2019–2020 (Exclude parents.) (FAFSA/SAR #74) ÷	
28. PARENTS' CONTRIBUTION (standard contribution for nine-month enrollment)*** If negative, enter zero. =	

**Do *not* include the family's home.

***To calculate the parents' contribution for other than nine-month enrollment, see page 11.

Continued on the next page.

	STUDENT'S INCOME IN 2017	
29.	Adjusted gross income (FAFSA/SAR #36) If negative, enter zero.	
30.	Income earned from work (FAFSA/SAR #39)	
31.	Taxable income (If tax filer, enter the amount from line 29 above. If non-tax filer, enter the amount from line 30.)	
32.	Total untaxed income and benefits (total of FAFSA/SAR #45a through 45j) +	
33.	Taxable and untaxed income (sum of line 31 and line 32) =	
34.	Total additional financial information (total of FAFSA/SAR #44a through 44f) −	
35.	TOTAL INCOME (line 33 minus line 34) = May be a negative number.	

	ALLOWANCES AGAINST STUDENT INCOME	
36.	2017 U.S. income tax paid (FAFSA/SAR #37) (tax filers only) If negative, enter zero.	
37.	State and other tax allowance (Table A7) If negative, enter zero. +	
38.	Social Security tax allowance (Table A2) +	
39.	Income protection allowance +	6,660
40.	Allowance for parents' negative adjusted available income (If line 25 is negative, enter line 25 as a positive number in line 40. If line 25 is zero or positive, enter zero in line 40.) +	
41.	TOTAL ALLOWANCES =	

	STUDENT'S CONTRIBUTION FROM INCOME	
	TOTAL INCOME (from line 35)	
	TOTAL ALLOWANCES (from line 41) −	
42.	Available income (AI) =	
43.	Assessment of AI ×	.50
44.	STUDENT'S CONTRIBUTION FROM AI = If negative, enter zero.	

	STUDENT'S CONTRIBUTION FROM ASSETS	
45.	Cash, savings, and checking (FAFSA/SAR #41)	
46.	Net worth of investments* (FAFSA/SAR #42) If negative, enter zero +	
47.	Net worth of business and/or investment farm (FAFSA/SAR #43) If negative, enter zero. +	
48.	Net worth (sum of lines 45 through 47) =	
49.	Assessment rate ×	.20
50.	STUDENT'S CONTRIBUTION FROM ASSETS =	

EXPECTED FAMILY CONTRIBUTION	
PARENTS' CONTRIBUTION (from line 28)	
STUDENT'S CONTRIBUTION FROM AI (from line 44) +	
STUDENT'S CONTRIBUTION FROM ASSETS (from line 50) +	
51. EXPECTED FAMILY CONTRIBUTION (standard contribution for nine-month enrollment)** If negative, enter zero. =	

*Do *not* include the student's home.

**To calculate the EFC for other than nine-month enrollment, see the next page.

Because savings or other assets in a child's name are generally counted at a *higher rate* than the savings or assets owned by a parent(s) (i.e. .20 instead of .12), if a choice exists as to who should own assets, the EFC will be lower if the parent(s) own them.

It is important to note a distribution can be taken from an IRA, including a Roth IRA, at any time. However, generally, a distribution can be taken from a 401(k) plan (including a Roth component thereof) only following severance of employment. Many 401(k) plans have loan features and/or hardship distribution features. A loan does not create income, but it does create assets.

There is a limited exemption for Section 529 assets and other investments when it comes to calculating federal financial aid for college. A section 529 plan generally provides for tax-free growth of assets and tax-free distributions of accumulated funds that are used for certain education costs. Income taxation and a 10 percent excise tax *generally* apply to earnings not used for permissible costs.

The Section 529 account assets of grandparents are not part of the assets component of the federal financial aid equation. However, distributions from such accounts are included in income for the FAFSA computations. In contrast, a distribution from a 529 account to a parent or the child is not included in income.

Section 529 account assets can be used to buy computer equipment and technology products. Also, distributed amounts used to pay tuition can be re-contributed within 60 days of receipt of a tuition refund (e.g. due to a scholarship) without taxation.

Planning Example. A family with young teenagers or younger children owns significant investment assets, and thought has been given to purchasing a larger home. The "upgrade" could help save on college costs. For example, a family with $450,000 of investments (e.g. stocks), $80,000 of Section 529 plan assets and two children born more than three years apart would reduce EFC by $8,460 for each year of college by using $150,000 of the stocks to upgrade the home (i.e. 150,000 x .12 x .47). Of course, if the stocks had appreciated in value, long-term capital gain would exist on the sale. The highest potential federal tax rate attributable thereto is 20 percent, but for many the rate is 0 percent. Higher earners could also be subject to the additional 3.8 percent tax on investment income. However, gain on the sale of a home generally is tax-free.

A home equity line of credit (HELOC) can be of significant value in the FAFSA analysis. Until it is drawn upon, no asset is created. If it is drawn upon and the amount borrowed is immediately expended (e.g. on education), there is no asset remaining for inclusion in FAFSA computations. (Loan proceeds are not income.)

Some schools may be willing to strike a deal on their portion of aid for the full four years of college. In this regard, people often wish to know what they're getting into up front, and some schools are sympathetic to the need. Striking a deal up front may be beneficial if net income or net worth is anticipated to increase substantially after the initial year of applying for aid. Also, it should be noted that not all colleges are equal and not all college aid is equal. Grants are worth much more than loans. Some schools will cover all or virtually all of the cost in excess of the EFC of students they accept.

Even if federal financial aid is not forthcoming, it likely is worthwhile to file the FAFSA. Colleges like to have a mix of "full-pays" and "partial-pays." Applying and not getting aid may help a child get accepted because of full-pay status. Also, merit aid is often only awarded with respect to students who apply for financial aid via filing a FAFSA. Filing is necessary to obtain low interest federal loans. Finally, if a family's situation changes, filing the FAFSA could make aid more accessible.

If a trust exists, income received from it is income for eligibility calculation purposes. The value of accumulated income or assets which the beneficiary can access generally must be included in assets, and the present value of corpus to be received in the future generally must be included in assets.

Interests owned in small businesses are excluded from the definition of "investments." For this purpose, a small business generally means a business with not more than 100 full-time or full-time equivalent employees that is owned and controlled by the family. Note the potential enormity of this exemption.

Rental real estate is included in assets. People might own a rental home and lease it directly to the tenant. For better liability protection, the home might be leased to an LLC or corporation, which in turn leases it to the tenant. If the real estate is owned by an LLC, it may qualify for the small business exemption. In this regard, the fact that a single member LLC is disregarded for federal income tax purposes generally has no bearing on other areas of law. However, a downside of having an LLC own and directly lease the property to the tenant is the property is more exposed to potential loss in the event of a lawsuit by the tenant (because the corporate veil would not need to be pierced if the property was owned by the LLC).

Planning Ideas. If earnings have been distributed by the business on an annual basis (or roughly on an annual basis) and invested by the owner, the business could instead retain the earnings and invest them. (Tax considerations should be taken into account.) The investment assets owned by the business should not be counted towards the investments total of the business owner for federal financial aid calculations purposes. Of course, there may be a concern about risk of loss due to the assets continuing to be held by the company. It *might* be possible to create a holding company to own the equity interests of the existing company, and have the existing company distribute the assets to the holding company (so that they would be safe from the operating company's creditors), without having the assets counted for federal financial aid purposes. It *might* also be possible to make a capital contribution of assets to a company, thereby reducing personal assets taken into account for purposes of the federal financial aid calculations. Careful thought and analysis would be necessary to ensure legality and cost-effectiveness before undertaking any such planning actions.

Gifts can be made to reduce assets and net worth. If a trusted person (e.g. the child's grandparent) exists who is very likely to someday return a gift, and there are absolutely no strings attached (such that the gift might not be returned), making a gift to a trusted person could make sense.

For self-employed persons, there may be a means of reducing income just before a child enters or children enter college and continuing the lower income throughout the college years, thereby minimizing the EFC. In recent years, tremendous deductions have been permitted with respect to depreciation of capital assets, such as equipment and software. As discussed in Chapter 5, many businesses are able to "expense" (i.e. immediately deduct the full costs of) capital asset purchases.

Certain retirement plans, such as a cash balance plan, can produce large tax-deductible contributions for highly paid individuals. Generally, a cash balance plan formula can be creative so as to provide for a relatively low allocation rate (e.g. 10 percent) for compensation up to a particular level (e.g. $40,000) and a high allocation rate with respect to compensation in excess thereof (e.g. 60

percent). Certain demographics must exist in order for a cash balance plan to work. An option here for a self-employed person who works alone might be to make an S election for the business (assuming it is an LLC or a corporation), pay the owner a reasonable salary, purchase capital assets (as needed), and establish a cash balance plan to require significant contributions during the college years. The plan might be frozen thereafter. Reasonable compensation would need to be paid. The contributions to the cash balance plan would be tax-deductible, thereby reducing taxes and increasing ACA credits eligibility. Depending on the facts, it might be possible to "zero out" the taxable income of the company. As noted in Chapter 5, an S election may not be advantageous after 2017, given the new Section 199A deduction. New Code section 199A needs to be considered. It is always best to "run the numbers."

For those who are self-employed and can do so, establishing an HSA with a high deductible health plan (HDHP) often makes sense. The contributions to the HSA would be tax-deductible. The health insurance premiums for the HDHP would be deductible for income tax purposes. While not entirely clear from existing authorities, it is likely that the HSA's assets would be excluded from the investments' total for purposes of federal financial aid for college. It is likely that the annual contributions would have to be added back when calculating income for any year. In contrast, it appears that contributions to a flexible spending account (FSA) would not need to be added back. A high deductible health plan is a plan that meets the requirement of Internal Revenue Code section 223(c)(2). Generally speaking, it provides for a minimum deductible ($1,350 for single coverage and $2,700 for family coverage for 2019) and places limits on maximum out-of-pocket costs for any given year ($6,750 for single coverage and $13,500 for family coverage for 2019). Distributions from HSAs that are used for health care purposes would not be counted.

If one's age is right, and Roth money exists to be withdrawn and sufficient retirement assets otherwise exist or will exist, it might make sense to borrow from a HELOC during college years, immediately pay for tuition and board with the borrowed funds, and later (after college) withdraw Roth funds to pay off any college loans.

Some quick pointers:

• Pay off bills immediately before completing FAFSA, so as to minimize cash accounts;
• Pay off credit cards and consumer debt with cash, as credit card and consumer debt balances do not reduce FAFSA assets;
• Pay down a mortgage or improve the home with excess liquid assets;
• If you own a small business that is exempt, leave money that is not currently needed in it; and
• If two children are in college at one time, EFC is generally cut in half (so, if one child is considering doing something else for a year, think about timing).

COMPARISON OF POSSIBLE FUNDING MEANS. The chart that follows this paragraph compares a 529 plan to a traditional IRA and a Roth IRA as a means of saving for college. The 2015-2016 FAFSA and the 2015 tax system are used for all purposes. The 2019 results would be substantially similar. The assumptions include: $108,000 of self-employment income, one working parent, bronze ACA exchange health coverage, maximum 401(k)/profit sharing, etc.) generally apply. Also, for each year, it is assumed that the family has $2,000 in cash and $40,000 in stocks, etc. held outside tax-qualified plans and IRAs. The resident state is Georgia. It is further assumed that the family wishes to save $100,000 in eight years, to be available for their daughter to attend college beginning in eight years. The daughter is a good student, so she should qualify for at least some scholarship money. The family believes it can earn five percent (5%) per year. Thus, eight years of $10,000 of payments should produce $100,265 of assets at the end of the eight year period. In the Roth and 529 plan analyses, the $10,000 annual contributions are funded by reductions to contributions to the self-employed person's tax-qualified plan. In the below analysis, assets were assumed to grow at five percent (5%) per year, and the accumulated assets were withdrawn by dividing the accumulated assets by the number of years of college remaining. The maximum federal education credits were deemed available during the years of college. The oldest parent is currently 48 years old. One child is presumed to be in college at all times, starting in 8 years. The chart shows that the cost of financing through a 529 plan is less than the costs of financing through a traditional IRA or a Roth IRA. Ordinarily, this will be the case. However, if the parents are in a relatively high tax bracket while working but will be in a relatively low bracket when the child is in college, such may not be the case.

Tax and FAFSA Combined Differences											
	Trad IRA:				529 Plan:				Roth:		
Year:	Tax	EFC	Combo	5% Disc	Tax	EFC	Combo	5% Disc	Tax	EFC	Combo	5% Disc
1	3064	0	3064	3064	120	0	120	120	0	0	0	0
2	3064	0	3064	2918	120	0	120	114	0	0	0	0
3	3064	0	3064	2785	120	0	120	109	0	0	0	0
4	3064	0	3064	2641	120	0	120	103	0	0	0	0
5	3064	0	3064	2511	120	0	120	98	0	0	0	0
6	3064	0	3064	2394	120	0	120	94	0	0	0	0
7	3064	0	3064	2287	120	0	120	90	0	0	0	0
8	3064	0	3064	2173	120	0	120	85	0	0	0	0
9	-10244	-576	-10820	-7311	0	-5655	-5655	-3821	0	0	0	0
10	-10244	-5638	-15882	-10246	0	0	0	0	0	-7293	-7293	-4705

11	-10244	-6974	-17218	-10563	0	0	0	0	0	-9262	-9262	-5682
12	-7,544	-8457	-16001	-9357	0	0	0	0	-7748	-11362	-19110	-11175
Totals	-13764	-21645	-35409	-16704	960	-5655	-4695	-3007	-7748	-27917	-35665	-21563

Note: One of the benefits of using an IRA is that if the money is not needed, it can be used in retirement. (With a Roth in the above analysis, all of the *income* distributed would ordinarily be tax-free in retirement.) In contrast, distributions of income from a 529 account that are not used for education purposes are ordinary income. Furthermore, a 10 percent penalty generally applies to income, subject to important exceptions for death and disability, and for amounts received as a scholarship.

ADVANCED PLANNING EXAMPLE

This example shows how a pension plan (i.e. not a 401(k) plan or a profit-sharing plan) can be utilized by a self-employed person to provide better benefits than a 529 plan: Joe owns and runs an LLC law firm. (A single member LLC is a disregarded entity for federal tax purposes. In other words, it is deemed not to exist, and the LLC's net income must be reported by the owner on Schedule C of his or her income tax return.) Joe is married and he and his wife have two children. Joe is age 52, is older than his spouse, and averages net income of $200,000 per year (excluding any retirement expenses). A few lawyers occasionally work for Joe's firm on a contract basis. Also assume: (a) Joe's spouse does not work; (b) the couple's two children are ages 16 and 14; (c) the couple's deductible itemized deductions for interest, taxes and charitable contributions total $20,000; (d) the couple has a home worth $350,000, a $50,000 Roth IRA, a $50,000 traditional IRA, $350,000 in a profit sharing/401(k) plan and $100,000 of Section 529 plan assets; and (e) HDHP and HSA coverage exist, with the

HDHP premiums being $1,200/month and the HSA contribution being $7,900. Also assume anticipated college costs will be $50,000 per year (although some will presumably be covered by grants and loans). The couple lives in Georgia, has excellent credit, and could qualify for a HELOC up to $300,000. The couple has been "maxing out" on Joe's profit sharing/401(k) plan through his firm's plan and making an IRA contribution for Joe's wife each year.

Options: As the children are getting close to college age, Joe and his wife are considering cutting Joe's retirement contributions back by eliminating profit sharing contributions each year for three years and investing the $30,000 saved each year in a 529 plan, and then returning to "maxing out" on retirement contributions at the end of the three year period. However, an alternative course of action has been proposed: Instead of the proposed course of action (i.e. investing $30,000/year in a 529 plan), (a) make an S election for the business, (b) pay a reasonable salary (e.g. $120,000), (c) establish a cash balance pension plan with a compensation credit of 60 percent of compensation, and (d) tap the HELOC to pay for college to the extent existing savings and future earnings are insufficient to cover costs. (A description of a cash balance plan and how it works can be found in Chapter 8.) For a year when net income before deduction of compensation and pension contributions was $200,000, the required cash balance plan contribution would be $72,000 (i.e. 60 percent of $120,000). The company would have a net loss of $1,180 [i.e. 200,000 − (120,000 + 72,000 + 9,180)]. ($9,180 is the company's FICA share.) If necessary to fund the pension plan, a cash capital contribution could be made.

Under the 529 approach, federal and state taxes (Georgia assumed, and including health care costs) are approximately $26,000 greater than under the cash balance plan approach for the first three years of the plan. Also, assuming a 5 percent rate of return, the EFC would be approximately $23,000 less for the first three years of college under the cash balance plan approach. Continued use of the cash balance plan thereafter (in lieu of switching back to regular profit sharing contributions) would produce similar (but not as great) results. Much more money will be saved for retirement through the cash balance plan. At age 59½ and thereafter, distributions therefrom (or from an IRA following rollover from the plan) would be subject to income tax but not subject to the 10 percent early withdrawal penalty of Code section 72(t). The cash balance approach is superior. Note: Running the numbers both ways will show the pros and cons of each approach.

Chapter 8

Saving For Retirement

Overview and Basic Retirement Plan Options

Overview. The main general benefit of saving for retirement is to have a comfortable retirement. Savings can be done basically two ways: With tax-favored plans and without tax-favored plans. A combination of both means is often used. Investments outside tax-favored plans include real estate. Social Security also supplies retirement benefits.

Tax-favored plans are tax-qualified retirement plans and individual retirement accounts (IRAs). A tax-qualified retirement plan (or tax-qualified plan) is a plan that meets the requirements of Internal Revenue Code section 401(a), 403(b) or 457(b). The main benefits of a tax-qualified plan are: (a) income tax deductions are generally available for plan contributions; (b) plan assets and earnings thereon grow tax-free; and (c) distributions can be "rolled over" to an IRA for further tax-free growth following retirement.

Depending on the plan terms and employer demographics, it is possible for one person to save hundreds of thousands to millions of dollars in tax-qualified plans and IRAs. However, the earlier a person begins saving, the more money there will be in retirement. As noted in Chapter 2, saving for retirement probably is the most favored activity under federal law. As noted in Chapter 3, it is the best asset protection mechanism.

The powers of compounding are astounding. Using five percent (5%) interest compounded annually, three

$3,000 investments made at ages 25, 30 and 35 will yield a greater sum at age 65 than three $10,000 investments made at ages 50, 55 and 60.

As noted in Chapter 3, even in bankruptcy, tax-qualified retirement plan assets are protected from creditors. Assets held in a nonqualified retirement plan (i.e. a retirement plan that is not tax-qualified) and non-retirement plan assets savings (in any form) generally are not protected from creditors. In bankruptcy, federal law protects all IRA rollover funds (i.e. assets transferred from tax-qualified plans) and IRA funds not sourced from tax-qualified plan rollovers to the extent of $1,283,025 (—in 2018; the amount originally was $1,000,000, but has been indexed for inflation since 2005). However, an inherited IRA's assets can be reached by the creditors of the death beneficiary in a bankruptcy situation. Means of protecting an inherited IRA's assets in the event of bankruptcy of a person who inherits an IRA are discussed in Chapter 3. (A death beneficiary "inherits" an IRA by being entitled to some or all of the IRA's assets following death of the IRA owner.)

With respect to IRAs, state law specifies protection outside bankruptcy. Georgia law provides that tax-qualified plan assets of plan participants and assets of IRAs (traditional and Roth) generally are protected from garnishment. An exception exists for alimony or child support.

Based on the historical tax system of the U.S., saving for retirement through tax-qualified plans and IRAs has been tax beneficial for the vast majority of the population. This is so because the assets of tax-qualified plans and IRAs generally grow tax-free and people have generally been in a higher incremental tax bracket while working than the incremental tax bracket applicable to them in retirement. However, for the reasons set forth in Chapter 1, it is not clear if this traditional rule of thumb regarding incremental tax brackets will hold true in the future. In this regard, the highest incremental income tax rates were much higher (i.e. well above 50 percent) in the 1940s-1970s than they are today. But, as noted in Chapter 2, seniors have tremendous political power, thus potentially providing them security. So, generally speaking, it makes sense to save for retirement through tax-qualified plans and IRAs.

Saving outside tax-qualified plans and IRAs makes sense as well, particularly if the assets will appreciate and be taxed on a favorable basis. For example, real estate (such as a rental home) generally produces capital gain upon sale. Many people successfully save using both tax-qualified plans/IRAs and assets owned outside tax-qualified plans and IRAs.

The "third leg" of the retirement stool—Social Security—should be considered. It is discussed in Chapter 9. To the extent it can be relied upon for future benefits, it will produce an income stream that is increased for inflation with annual cost-of-living adjustments (COLAs).

General Retirement Plan Options. Only an employer or a self-employed person can maintain a tax-qualified retirement plan. Thus, if a person works only as an employee (as most people do), his/her employer will determine the terms and availability of tax-qualified plans and perhaps other retirement plans in which the person can participate. However, a self-employed person can create any type tax-qualified plan that he or she desires. The same holds true for an LLC, S corporation or a partnership, because they can constitute an employer. Any individual can establish an IRA for himself or herself.

As explained below, limits exist on the ability of individuals to make tax-deductible IRA contributions and (nondeductible) Roth IRA contributions.

So, if a person works only as an employee, he will receive his retirement plan options from his or her employer. The most common employer plan used today is a 401(k) plan. And, 401(k) plans ordinarily provide for matching contributions. As an almost absolute rule, persons who can afford to take make contributions to a 401(k) plan and thereby receive any sort of significant matching contributions should do so. Unless the contributions are Roth contributions, making such contributions reduces one's taxable income for income tax purposes. Elective deferral contributions to 401(k) plans are added back to income when analyzing college aid eligibility but are not added back for Obamacare purposes. Generally, a person who works only as an employee can also make IRA contributions.

For someone who is self-employed, either fully or partially, the retirement plan options are potentially much greater than those available to someone who works only as an employee. Self-employed persons generally include partners and LLC members. For those situations, the partnership or LLC will generally establish the retirement plan(s) for the partnership or LLC. Generally, the partners and members can also make IRA contributions outside the plans established by the partnership or LLC. For pure self-employed persons (i.e. those who solely own a business), the retirement plan options and flexibility are greatest. These options are described below.

Summary of Federal Retirement Plan Rules

Basics. A tax-qualified plan is one that meets the requirements of section 401(a) of the Internal Revenue Code. An IRA is an account for a person that meets the requirements of section 408 of the Internal Revenue Code. A 401(k) plan meets the requirements of Code section 401(k) and the applicable provisions of Code section 401(a).

Certain non-discrimination rules apply to tax-qualified plans. They exist to ensure that a minimum percent of employees who are not owners or highly paid employees of the business participate in the plan, and that the benefits such persons receive are reasonably in line with the benefits received by the owners and highly paid employees. Also, limits exist on these tax-subsidized benefits.

When an employee terminates employment (but generally not before then), a retirement plan often permits the employee to receive his or her vested benefits. Those benefits can then be "rolled over" on a tax-free basis to another tax-qualified retirement plan (if the other plan will accept the "roll-in") or to an IRA. A few pension plans do not permit lump-sum distributions. Rather, the only benefit form is a life annuity. For married persons, the spouse must ordinarily consent to a death benefit distribution to someone other than him or her.

Similar to a tax-qualified plan, only employers and self-employed persons can establish and maintain a similar plan involving IRAs such as a Simplified Employee Pension (SEP). SEPs are discussed further below. Ordinarily, an owner of a single member LLC, a member of a multiple member LLC and a partner in a partnership would each be considered a self-employed person.

There are two types of tax-qualified plans: defined contribution ("DC") plans and defined benefit ("DB") plans. In a DC plan, each participant has his/her own account that grows with employer contributions and investment gains, and diminishes due to investment losses and distributions. Contributions are determined and/or allocated by a formula specified in the plan. In a DB plan, benefits are determined by a formula. Each participant is entitled to an accrued benefit—generally, a monthly benefit beginning at normal retirement age. A typical normal retirement age is 65.

Often, much greater tax-deductible contributions can be made to a DB plan than those that can be made to a DC plan, as a DB plan has a normal retirement age annuity limit equal to the lesser of $225,000 and the average compensation of the participant over his highest three calendar years preceding retirement. In 2019, a DC plan has an annual allocation limit generally equal to the lesser of 100 percent of compensation and $56,000. (The DB and DC limits are annually adjusted for inflation).

Most private sector retirement plans are governed by the Employee Retirement Income Security Act of 1974 (ERISA). This federal law preempts (overrides) most state laws that would regulate retirement plans. When ERISA was enacted, DB plans were prevalent. Now, DC plans are prevalent and, by far, the 401(k) plan is the most popular DC plan.

ERISA has both a Labor Code aspect to it and an Internal Revenue Code aspect to it, but the two aspects overlap tremendously. Thus, most retirement plans that are governed by ERISA are tax-qualified plans, so that the tax benefits of deductible contributions, asset security (i.e. held in trust apart from the employer and all creditors), tax-free growth and beneficial tax options upon distribution are received.

Discrimination Rules. To be tax-qualified, a plan must generally provide benefits to a reasonable percentage of nonhighly compensated employees ("NHCE"s) of the employer, when viewed compared to the percentage of highly compensated employees ("HCE"s) who benefit, and the benefits supplied to such NHCEs must be reasonably in line with the benefits provided to the HCEs. NHCEs are employees who are not HCEs. For 2019, HCEs are employees who made more than $120,000 in 2018 or are or were a five percent (5%) or greater owner in 2018 or 2019.

Regarding participation, the percentage of NHCEs eligible to participate generally must equal or exceed 70 percent of the percentage of HCEs eligible to participate. However, using the more liberal "average benefit percentage" test, the percent can drop much lower (the lowest percent possible is 20 percent), provided the average benefit for the NHCEs for the year equals or exceeds 70 percent of the average benefit of the HCEs. A participant's benefit percentage is either his normal retirement annual benefit increase or the combination of increases to his account other than earnings or interest income, divided by his compensation. For purposes of running these tests, various employees can be excluded from the analysis, including certain part-time employees.

Concerning nondiscrimination with respect to benefits, a DC plan *generally* must provide for a common allocation rate of compensation for all participants (e.g. 3 percent of compensation) and the definition of compensation must be reasonable. The allocation rate can vary from year-to-year if the plan is a profit sharing plan. As discussed below, allocation formulas other than pro rata based on compensation can be used.

For a profit sharing plan that includes a 401(k) component, a different discrimination test applies to the 401(k) component. Unless the plan is a safe harbor plan, it must pass the ADP and ACP tests. Generally, (a) under the ADP test, the average of the deferral ratios for the HCE participants must not be more than two percentage points greater than, nor more than double, the average of the deferral ratios for the NHCE participants, and (b) under the ACP test, the average of the matching contributions ratios for the HCE participants must not be two percentage points greater than, nor more than double, the average of the matching contributions ratios for the NHCE participants. A deferral ratio is a participant's 401(k) contributions divided by his compensation. Generally, a contributions ratio is a participant's matching contributions divided by his compensation for the year.

For a DB plan, looking at individuals or groups of employees, the annual accrual rate (i.e. growth in the normal retirement benefit as a percentage of current compensation) for NHCE participants must equal or exceed the rate applicable to HCE participants on a nondiscriminatory basis. If all participants have the same accrual rate, the DB plan will automatically be nondiscriminatory in terms of benefits provided. However, other more aggressive plan terms can be used to provide greater accrual rates to HCEs who are older, on average, than the NHCEs who participate.

While DC plans ordinarily are tested for discrimination on a contributions basis (i.e. employer contributions for the year divided by the participant's compensation) and DB plans are generally tested on a benefit accrual basis (i.e. additional benefit accrual for the year divided by participant's compensation), under "cross-testing," a DC plan can be tested on a benefit accrual basis (instead of a contributions basis) and a DB plan can be tested on a contributions basis. Cross-testing involves converting contribution percentages to benefit accrual percentages, and vice-versa. Cross-testing is often beneficial when the HCEs, as a group, are significantly older than the NHCEs, as a group, and a desire exists to provide greater contributions or benefits (relative to compensation) to the older HCEs.

Distributions. Generally speaking, distributions from a tax-qualified plan can only be made after a participant terminates employment. Over the years, significant issues have existed about when termination of employment or "separation from service" occurs. At one time, 401(k) plans could permit distribution of benefits only upon a "separation from service." Now, distributions can be made following severance from employment.

Generally, a tax-qualified plan does not have to permit distribution of benefits upon termination of employment. A pension plan could, for example, only allow for benefits to be paid beginning at normal retirement age (often, age 65). But, most plans permit distributions following termination of employment. A pension plan distribution made following termination of employment (assuming it is a lump-sum) would ordinarily be the discounted present value of the future vested accrued benefit (i.e. anticipated future monthly payments) at the time of termination of employment. Thus, interest rates can have a significant impact on pension plan lump-sums. For a 401(k) profit sharing plan, the vested account balance ordinarily would be distributable. As an almost absolute rule, benefits can be partially or wholly rolled over to an IRA.

In addition to allowing distributions upon termination of employment, 401(k) plans often permit in-service hardship distributions. And, some profit sharing plans (or profit sharing components of 401(k) profit sharing plans) allow for distributions of employer-provided benefits (i.e. not elective deferrals or earnings thereon) while still employed, upon attainment of a particular age or after a stated event occurs (e.g. sale of the company). The IRS has stated that distribution of employer-funded profit sharing money can be made after five years of participation, or after two or more years of funds accumulation.

Benefits Limits. There are annual limits on contributions to a DC plan and limits on benefits that a DB plan can provide. Code section 415 sets the limits. For 2019, the DC limit is the lesser of compensation earned or $56,000. An additional $6,000 can be contributed to a 401(k) plan by a person age 50+ by year-end, bringing the total to $62,000 for such a person. For a DB plan, the maximum life annuity that can be received at normal retirement age generally is the lesser of $225,000 or 100 percent of the average compensation of the participant over the highest three years of being paid. Deduction and funding rules permit and require the life annuity to be funded over a reasonable time span.

Under the deduction limits of Code section 404, generally, no more than 25 percent of the combined compensation of all DC plan participants can be contributed to a DC plan for a year on a tax-deductible basis. However, 401(k) elective deferrals are not taken into account for this purpose, meaning they can be contributed in addition to 25 percent of combined compensation. For a DB plan, the amount that can be contributed for a year will ordinarily be an actuarially determined range with a high number and a low number. The high number is the most that can be contributed on a tax-deductible basis. The low number is the amount that must be contributed to avoid excise taxes applicable to underfunding. Ordinarily, actuaries compute the numbers. Under Code section 4972, a ten percent (10%) excise tax applies to contributions in excess of deduction limits.

For purposes of discrimination testing, distributions, and tax-deductible contributions limitations, affiliated employers are treated as one employer. The affiliated employer rules are complex. Generally speaking, they require companies with 80 percent or greater common ownership to be treated as one company. In some cases, where a few individuals, estates or trusts own the companies, the affiliation standard drops to greater than 50 percent. Additional affiliation rules apply to professional service businesses. Also, leased employees must be taken into account by the lessee. Generally, a leased employee is someone who is under the primary direction or control of the plan sponsor but on the payroll of another company, and has been in such a position for a year or more.

Vesting. Employee contributions to tax-qualified plans must be non-forfeitable (i.e. vested) at all times. Benefits of participants that are supplied by employer contributions must be vested within a statutorily-specified period of time or shorter. Code section 411 specifies that DB plans must ordinarily apply a 5-year cliff vesting schedule or a 3-7 year graded vesting schedule. With a 5-year cliff vesting schedule, the vested percent is zero until five years of service have been performed. Thereafter, the vested percent is 100. With a 3-7 year graded vesting schedule, benefits vest in 20 percent increments between years 3 through 7 of employment. DC plans generally must use a 3-year cliff vesting schedule or a 2-6 year graded vesting schedule.

Generally, all years of service after a plan is adopted must be taken into account. A year of service is, generally speaking, a year in which 1,000 or more hours of service are performed. Prior service (i.e. before plan adoption) may be included for purposes of vesting or it may be excluded, but if included, it must be granted on a nondiscriminatory basis.

Plans can forfeit non-vested benefits when a participant takes a distribution of his benefits following termination of employment. However, if a plan provides for such forfeitures, it must allow the participant's benefit to be "bought back" upon return to service within a specified period of time (generally, 5 years). For a fully non-vested benefit, it can be deemed to have be distributed (i.e. "cashed out"), provided a deemed buy-back occurs if the participant returns within a specified period of time (generally, 5 years).

Common Retirement Plans

401(k) Plan. Most large employers have moved to 401(k) plans with either matching contributions or a safe harbor contribution formula. Safe harbor contributions (generally 3 percent of compensation) are fully vested, but using them eliminates the need to run the ADP/ACP tests ordinarily applicable to 401(k) plans. In lieu of a 3 percent contribution, a safe harbor plan can provide for fully vested dollar-for-dollar matching contributions on the first three percent deferred by a participant plus fifty cents on the next two percent deferred by the participant.

The take-off of 401(k) plans has been one of the greatest boons for employers—employees pay most of the cost of their retirement benefits. Many plans have an automatic enrollment feature, whereby participation occurs at a specified deferral rate (often, 3 percent) absent action by the participant to prevent the deferrals. A safe harbor 401(k) plan can be attractive to small and mid-sized businesses where lower income employees do not substantially participate in making 401(k) deferrals.

Often, 401(k) plans include loan features. A loan feature permits a participant to receive a loan while working. A loan feature can help a participant get through a short-term period of difficulty on a tax-free basis.

Since 2006, 401(k) plans have been permitted to allow Roth contributions. Unlike traditional 401(k) contributions, Roth 401(k) contributions do not reduce compensation income for income tax purposes. However, as long as certain holding requirements are met, distributions from a Roth 401(k) account are tax-free to the "distributee." The amount of Roth 401(k) contributions a participant can make is the ordinary 401(k) deferral limit ($19,000 for 2019; $25,000 if age 50+), less the amount of traditional 401(k) elective deferral contributions made. Once a Roth elective deferral is made to a 401(k) plan, it cannot be reversed. A 401(k) plan can allow a traditional 401(k) account to be partially or wholly converted to a Roth account. Ordinary income is recognized upon the conversion. Roth accounts in 401(k) plans can be rolled over to a Roth IRA following termination of employment.

Virtually always, a 401(k) plan will include a profit sharing component in addition to the 401(k) component. The profit sharing component allows the employer to make contributions to be allocated to separate profit sharing accounts. Generally, up to 25 percent of the total compensation of all plan participants can be contributed on a tax-deductible basis. Elective deferrals to 401(k) plans, etc. are excluded from the amounts subject to these limits. There are a few permissible means of allocating the contribution to accounts of participants.

They are discussed below. A simple 401(k) plan can also be adopted. However, as the ability to defer is less, this plan is not popular.

Cash Balance Plan. Cash balance plans (or cash balance pension plans) are often used by law firms and physicians' practices to maximize benefits for owner professionals while providing relatively small benefits for staff employees. Groups of employees are either covered or excluded. A cash balance plan is a DB plan, but it looks like a DC plan to participants. Each participant has a hypothetical "account," and his plan benefit is an accrued benefit that is ordinarily denominated in the form of a lump-sum amount.

The initial hypothetical account in a cash balance plan is increased by a benefit credit that ordinarily is a percentage of plan compensation. The account also grows by an interest or earnings factor. A five percent interest rate might apply. So, for example, if a compensation credit was 10 percent, a participant who earned $100,000 would have an account balance of $10,000 after the first year of plan operation if a beginning balance did not exist via plan terms. If the interest rate was 5 percent, the account would grow by 5 percent to $10,500 by the next annual benefit accrual allocation date.

The actual earnings rate of the trust will be a factor in determining how much can or must be contributed to the plan for any given year. As actuarially computed, the plan must have enough assets to pay future benefits. So, actual plan assets (and the earnings and losses that produce them) will impact funding requirements and limitations.

Because a cash balance plan is a DB plan, the ordinary benefit form must be a life annuity. If the participant is married, the life annuity generally must be a joint and survivor life annuity wherein the surviving spouse's benefit equals or exceeds 50 percent of the participant's life annuity benefit. However, with spousal consent, this form of benefit can be waived and a lump-sum or other available distribution form taken.

Cash balance plans work well when the owners (or other group desired to receive substantial benefits) are significantly older, as a group, than the other plan participants. The plan is tested for discrimination by growing the compensation credit by a reasonable plan interest rate (e.g. 6 percent), converting the grown amount to a life annuity, and then dividing the life annuity amount by the current compensation of the participant. The life annuity amount-to-compensation ratios for the HCEs and the NHCEs must be reasonably in line. Generally, a minimum compensation credit rate of at least 5 percent must be supplied to NHCE participants. An example of how a cash balance plan is tested for discrimination is supplied below. A cash balance plan is often combined with a 401(k) plan (often, a safe harbor 401(k) plan) to provide the greatest deduction and deferral opportunities.

Cash Balance Plan Testing Example:

Doctor A owns a P.C. that employs two staff employees. Doctor A is age 60, and his staff employees are ages 40 and 25. The 40 year-old staff member makes $50,000/year and the 25 year-old staff member makes $35,000/year.

Doctor A's P.C. adopts a cash balance plan that covers all three employees; the benefit formula is 7 percent of compensation for non-physician employees and 50 percent of compensation for physicians; the plan uses a fixed 6 percent interest rate factor; plan compensation is capped under Code §401(a)(17) at $280,000 for 2019

(Doctor A earns more than this amount); the normal retirement age is 65

Doctor A's benefit: 280,000 x .50 = **140,000**; discrimination analysis: 140,000 x 1.06 to the fifth power = 187,352; 187,352/280,000 = .669

Age 40 Employee's benefit: 50,000 x .07 = **3,500**; discrimination analysis: 3,500 x 1.06 to the 25th power = 15,015; 15,015/50,000 = .300

Age 25 Employee's benefit: 35,000 x .07 = **2,450**; discrimination analysis: 2,450 x 1.06 to the 40th power = 25,211; 25,211/35,000 = .720

Under this example, one of the two NHCEs has an allocation rate equal to or greater than the HCE's allocation rate[5]. Under section 410(b) regulations, this ratio (50 percent—i.e. ((1/2)/(1/1))) is then tested to see if it passes the applicable tests; this plan should pass all of the nondiscrimination tests *(END EXAMPLE)*

Some general cash balance plan rules and other considerations:

-A 3 year cliff vesting schedule (or shorter) applies

-Particularly if there is more than one HCE owner, investments should be done conservatively (and long-term bonds may now be risky), because the employer is liable for any underfunding, and each participant is entitled to his/her benefit

---

[5] Technically, the deemed lump-sum amount is supposed to be converted to a life annuity, and the life annuity amount is analyzed as a percent of compensation. However, because uniform life expectancies are applied, the result will be the same whether this step is followed or not.

-generally, at least 40 percent of full-time employees must be covered

-like all other tax-qualified plans, the plan cannot discriminate in terms of hiring, firing, etc. based on age; however, absent an employment agreement, etc. to the contrary, it can limit future raises (or not make them) and instead make contributions to the plan

-although these plans are DB pension plans, PBGC premiums ordinarily are not required for small plans of professionals

-an actuary ordinarily is needed for annual funding analysis, etc. (but small plans generally have low costs)

-subject to limitations, the contribution percentage can increase once compensation hits a threshold, to deal with bad financial years; e.g. the compensation credit formula could be 10 percent up to $100,000 of compensation and 80 percent for compensation of $100,000 or more

-as a pension plan, a cash balance plan must provide "definitely determinable benefits;" thus, it cannot be regularly amended to change the benefits formula; there is no rule of thumb on how often such a plan can be amended.

As noted in the example provided at the end of Chapter 7, relating to Federal Financial Aid for College, an added benefit of a cash balance plan is the benefit accrual for the preceding year likely does not need to be added back to income when calculating the expected family contribution (EFC).

Age-Weighted Profit Sharing Plan. An age-weighted profit sharing plan is ordinarily designed to provide greater benefits for owners than those provided to non-owner employees. Similar to a cash balance plan, such a plan works well when the group for which substantial benefits are desired (generally, the owners) is substantially older than the other employees. However, this plan is a DC plan. Because this plan is a DC plan, there are annual limits on individual contributions that do not exist for cash balance plans. For 2019, total allocations, including 401(k) contributions but *not* including catch-up contributions, cannot exceed $56,000. Catch-up contributions of $6,000 can be made to a 401(k) account (so, the total maximum contribution is $62,000 for a participant age 50+ at year-end). Because a cash balance plan is a DB plan, ordinarily, the potential maximum deductible contributions that can be made to it will exceed $62,000 with respect to any owner who is middle age or older.

An example of an age-weighted formula for a physicians' practice might be 12 percent allocations for physicians, up to the plan compensation maximum of $280,000, and a 5 percent allocation for staff employees. Certain numbers would need to be run to make sure the nondiscrimination tests were met.

Age-weighted profit sharing plans are simpler than cash balance plans. Cross testing rules are applied to pass the nondiscrimination tests. Although it is generally not possible to contribute and deduct as much with an age-weighted profit sharing plan as is possible with a cash balance plan, many people are satisfied with less, particularly given the lesser costs involved. (Ordinarily, actuarial services aren't needed.)

A relatively popular formula for an age-weighted profit sharing plan is to use a 3 percent safe harbor 401(k) plan, with another 2 percent contribution being made to the profit sharing component for staff employees. The 3 percent contribution would be fully vested, but a vesting schedule could apply to the 2 percent contribution. A greater profit sharing contribution would be made for the highly paid employees. One plan could "house" both features. The benefit of a safe harbor 401(k) plan is that the ADP/ACP tests are deemed passed, meaning the HCEs could contribute the maximum 401(k) amount ($19,000 for 2019; $25,000 if 50+) and testing would not be required. For purposes of profit sharing discrimination testing, the NHCEs would each be deemed to have received a five percent (5%) allocation.

All profit sharing plans must provide recurring and substantial contributions. However, contributions need not be made annually. Subject to the discrimination requirements, the allocation formula could be x percent for staff employees and 2x for others, with x being a percent of compensation.

Traditional Profit Sharing Plan. A traditional profit sharing plan provides a single percent of compensation as the allocation to all participants' accounts (e.g. 7 percent). The annual percent can be fixed or it can vary. (Varying is more common.) So, if a seven percent contribution was made, a participant with $100,000 of plan compensation would receive an allocation (and contribution) of $7,000. The plan's definition of compensation must be nondiscriminatory. Derivatives of Form W-2 compensation work. The contribution/allocation percent ordinarily is discretionary, such that the employer contribution and the allocation percentage (to accounts) can vary each year. However, the allocation rate must be the same for each participant in any given year. This plan is *simple*. It can be attractive if the owners are not, as a group, substantially older than the staff. The profit sharing plan is usually coupled with a 401(k) plan.

Another variant on the traditional profit sharing plan is to provide the same contribution amount for all participants. This formula can provide value if the plan will be aggregated with a cash balance plan that provides a fixed interest rate credit, because a relatively high interest credit (up to 8.5 percent) can applied to these benefits when doing cross-testing.

Integrated Profit Sharing Plan. If the HCEs are not, as a group, substantially older than the staff, then an integrated profit sharing plan (ordinarily coupled with a 401(k) plan) provides a means of providing greater benefits for the owners, as a percent of compensation, than those provided to staff members under a traditional formula. However, the differential is not as great as the differentials that can be provided by a cash balance plan or an age-weighted profit sharing plan when the HCEs are, as a group, significantly older than the staff employees.

The allocation rate under an integrated profit sharing plan can increase with respect to compensation in excess of the "integration level," but it cannot be double or more than double the base rate, and it cannot exceed the base rate plus 5.7 percent. The integration level is an amount of compensation. It cannot exceed (but could be less than) the Social Security Wage Base (SSWB—$132,900 for 2019). A sample formula integrated profit sharing formula would be: 5 percent of compensation up to the SSWB plus 10 of compensation above the SSWB. The DC plan contribution plan annual limits outlined above apply to any profit sharing plan, regardless of the allocation formula. As noted, the profit sharing allocation formula (traditional or integrated) is often combined with 401(k) benefits, including matching contributions. The 401(k) component could be a safe harbor 401(k) plan. The formula can be fixed or flexible, in terms of required annual contributions.

Governmental and Tax-Exempt Employers' Plans. Tax-exempt employers and public schools and universities can maintain a 403(b) plan. State and local governments and tax-exempt employers can maintain a 457(b) plan. Public schools and universities often provide both type plans. These plans are very similar to 401(k) plans, except the discrimination rules are different. The ADP and ACP tests do not apply. However, the same elective deferral limits, including catch-up contribution limits, apply to each plan type. Under Code section 402(g), each individual has an annual personal limit on the amount of elective deferrals he can make to a 401(k) plan or a 403(b) plan. (The limit for 2019 is $19,000; $25,000 if age 50+.) However, an identical separate limit applies to a 457(b) plan. Thus, for an eligible employer that maintains both a 403(b) plan and a 457(b) plan, a participant can defer up to a total of $38,000 for a year ($50,000 if age 50+).

IRA-Based Plans. IRAs are discussed below. However, as many small employers maintain IRA-based plans, such plans are discussed here. Simplified employee pensions (SEPs) and Simple IRAs are not tax-qualified plans. Rather, they involve an employer setting up IRA accounts for employees, to which tax-deductible contributions can be made. Unlike most tax-qualified plans, full vesting is required at all times. However, these plans generally are not subject to ERISA (although ERISA's enforcement and fiduciary duties ordinarily apply), so a summary plan description (SPD) need not be supplied. A notice of plan benefits, etc. is required to be supplied to participants. Because benefits are held in IRAs, unlike tax-qualified plans, employees can take distributions at any time.

A SEP is like a profit sharing plan, except the formula must be either pro rata based on compensation or pro rata integrated. An IRS model form can be used to adopt a SEP. However, the IRS's model form does not permit integration. The annual individual contribution limit is the lesser of $56,000 or 25 percent compensation. The maximum compensation figure for 2019 is $280,000.

SEP eligibility can be limited to people age 21 or older who have worked for the employer in at least 3 of the preceding 5 years and have received at least $600 of compensation. Union employees and nonresident aliens can be excluded. Unlike tax-qualified plans, loans are not permitted. A SEP can be adopted as late as the due date of the employer's tax return, plus any extensions. Contributions may be made by as late as that date.

Similar to a 401(k) plan, a simple IRA is like a safe harbor 401(k) plan, except the required employer contributions are less and the amount employees can contribute is less. The deferral limit is $13,000 for 2019, plus a potential catch-up of $3,000. Employees making less than $5,000 generally can be excluded. The required employer contributions are either a 2 percent contribution or dollar-for-dollar matching contributions up to 3 percent of pay, except the 3 percent can be lowered to as low as 1 percent for not more than 2 calendar years in any 5 calendar year period.

A simple IRA plan must be adopted before elective deferral contributions can be made (and deferrals must be elected before they can be made). The employer contributions can be made by as late as the due date of the employer's income tax return (including extensions). At a minimum, employees must be given a 60 day window before each calendar year to make their deferral elections. Loans are not permitted.

Plan Trends. For the reasons noted above, the main trend has been towards 401(k) plans. And, safe harbor 401(k) plans have become very popular. Automatic enrollment and automatic escalations of deferral rates are commonplace, as inertia often prevents employees from acting to override. The automatic features are designed to increase participation and benefit accrual—two things ordinarily beneficial to employees.

With the exception of cash balance plans, DB plans continue their slow demise. There is little upside to these plans for large employers. If the plans does well in terms of investments, a 50 percent excise tax and income tax applies to a reversion of plan assets to the employer plan sponsor upon plan termination. Also, employees have often sued to access a reversion. Generally, these plans now only exist with respect to a few large employers and in the governmental sector. Often, the large employer plans are union plans. Many DB plans have been frozen and replaced by 401(k) plans or cash balance plans.

Individual Retirement Accounts (IRAs)

An IRA is an individual retirement account described in Internal Revenue Code section 408. The requirements to be an IRA are:

- Only cash contributions are permissible
- The trustee or custodian is a bank or other person who meets IRS requirements
- Assets cannot be invested in life insurance
- The beneficiary's interest must be fully vested
- The assets must be held in a separate account or otherwise segregated from non-IRA assets
- Except Roth IRAs, minimum required distributions are necessary following attainment of age $70\frac{1}{2}$

Under Code §408(m), subject to some possible exceptions (including possibly investment through a partnership), an IRA is deemed to distribute (upon purchase) any work of art, rug, antique, metal, gem, stamp or coin.

Distributions from a traditional IRA are taxable as ordinary income. Unlike a tax-qualified plan, distributions can be taken from an IRA at any time. However, with certain important exceptions, including attainment of age 59½, death and disability, distributions are subject to a ten percent (10%) penalty. Also unlike tax-qualified plans, there is no requirement that a spouse consent to a non-spouse death beneficiary.

There are two types of IRAs: traditional IRAs and Roth IRAs. A traditional IRA generally is created either by tax-deductible contributions to a traditional IRA or via transfer (rollover) of assets from a tax-qualified plan to a traditional IRA. A Roth IRA is an IRA created by non-deductible contributions to the Roth IRA, conversion of a traditional IRA to a Roth IRA, rollover of Roth funds from a 401(k) plan or rollover of pre-tax funds from a 401(k) plan to a Roth IRA (upon which ordinary income is recognized).

Rollovers can be done one of two ways: (1) receipt of the assets and transfer to a "rollee" within 60 days; or (2) a trustee-to-trustee transfer from "roller" institution to "rollee" institution. For the former type, once undertaken, another such transaction can be taken only after a year passes. For the latter type, an unlimited number of transfers can take place.

Traditional IRAs. If an individual is eligible to participate in a tax-qualified retirement plan, or if the individual's spouse is eligible to participate in an employer plan, the ability to participate in a traditional IRA for the year on a tax-deductible basis may be limited.

157

Generally, any working individual can contribute the lesser of their earned income or $6,000 to an IRA. For this purpose, earned income generally includes alimony. If the person will be age 50 or greater at year-end, an additional $1,000 catch-up contribution can be made. Such contributions generally are tax-deductible for income tax purposes. However, to be tax-deductible for a year, an IRA contribution must be made by April 15th of the following year. Excess contributions are not deductible and are subject to a six percent (6%) excise tax.

The ability to deduct a contribution can potentially be diminished or lost with respect to a person who actively participates in a tax-qualified plan of his employer if the person's income (or the joint income of the person and his or her spouse, if married and a joint return will be filed) exceeds a certain threshold. Generally speaking, a person actively participates in a tax-qualified plan for a year if he makes a contribution to the plan or receives a benefit accrual increase under the plan. For a joint return, generally (subject to income limits), the spouse of a person who participates in a tax-qualified plan can contribute $6,000 (plus another $1,000 if age 50 or older) to an IRA on a tax-deductible basis.

A single person who actively participates in a tax-qualified plan can deduct the lesser of the contribution limit ($6,000 or $7,000 for 2019) or the deduction limit. The deduction limit phases out for 2019 with respect to modified AGI between $64,000 and $74,000. (So, at $74,000 of modified AGI, a deductible IRA contribution cannot be made by an active participant single person.) Modified AGI generally means AGI.

If both spouses of a married couple that files a joint return actively participate in tax-qualified plans, the ability to make deductible contributions phases out between

$103,000 and $123,000 of modified AGI for 2019 through a complex equation. (The phase-out applies to the $6,000 or $7,000 contribution limit.) The lesser paid active participant spouse can deduct the lesser of the contribution limit, as adjusted due to the modified AGI active participation limit, or the sum of the compensation of the lesser paid spouse and the compensation of the higher paid spouse minus the combination of any IRA deduction for the higher paid spouse, the amount of designated nondeductible IRA contributions by the higher paid spouse and any Roth IRA contributions made by the higher paid spouse. If only one spouse of a couple that files jointly actively participates in a tax-qualified plan, the ability of the other spouse to make a tax-deductible contribution phases out between $193,000 and $203,000 of modified AGI. The other spouse need not have earned compensation to able to make such an IRA contribution.

Roth IRAs. A Roth IRA is an after-tax IRA. No tax deduction is available for contributions to a Roth IRA. However, provided certain time holding requirements are met, distributions from a Roth IRA are received completely tax-free.

Just as it is good for one's asset portfolio to be diversified, having some Roth money saved for retirement makes sense if the Roth money can be obtained at a reasonable price. Roth assets can be obtained by making Roth contributions to a Roth IRA or by converting a traditional IRA to a Roth IRA. As noted, 401(k) plans may also permit Roth contributions. They may also permit conversion of pre-tax 401(k) accounts to Roth 401(k) accounts.

Is it a good idea to make a Roth IRA contribution when a tax-deductible traditional IRA contribution could instead be made? And, when is it prudent to make a Roth conversion of a traditional IRA? These questions are very complex, and necessitate guesstimates of the fate of the country and the future tax system, as well as a determination of the individual's expectations in terms of future earnings and wealth. However, if one can make a Roth conversion at little or no tax cost, the person anticipates being a middle income or better earner over the remainder of a long future career, and the system will survive (see Chapter 1), then the odds of a Roth conversion being a bad choice are small. Using similar assumptions, if a traditional IRA contribution will produce little or no tax benefit, making a Roth contribution (instead) would likely be prudent if the person anticipates being a middle income or better earner over the remainder of a long future career.

A Roth IRA contribution of up to $6,000 ($7,000 if age 50 or older by year-end) can be made as long as modified AGI does not exceed $122,000 for single filers or $193,000 for married persons filing jointly. The ability to make Roth contributions phases out for single filers with modified AGI between $122,000 and $137,000. The phase-out for married persons filing jointly runs to $203,000. Some advocate a "back door" Roth if income is too high for a Roth contribution to be made, whereby a non-deductible contribution is made and then converted. Care should be exercised with a backdoor Roth conversion, particularly if a traditional IRA exists.

Unlike a traditional IRA, contributions to a Roth IRA can be made after attaining age 70½. And, pre-death minimum required distributions (MRDs) are not required.

Since 2010, anyone can make a Roth IRA conversion of a traditional IRA. However, ordinary income (but no 10 percent penalty) must be recognized upon the conversion. Pre-tax qualified plan benefits can be rolled to a Roth IRA when the benefits are distributable, provided that ordinary income must be recognized upon the conversion.

While the ten percent (10%) penalty of IRC section 72(t) generally applies only to income amounts distributed from a Roth IRA, if a Roth conversion occurs and the 5-year rule (discussed below) has not been met, the ten percent penalty will apply to the entire conversion amount (to the extent distributed) unless an exception to the penalty applies (e.g. attainment of age 59½).

Any "qualified distribution" from a Roth IRA or Roth 401(k) account is completely tax-free. A qualified distribution is one made due to death, disability or attainment of age 59½, and made after the person has satisfied the five year requirement. For a Roth IRA, a distribution made to a first time homebuyer also potentially qualifies if the five year requirement is met. The five year requirement is met with respect to a Roth IRA if the distribution is made after the end of the 5-year period beginning on the first day of the first year in which a Roth contribution was made to any Roth IRA. A similar rule applies to Roth 401(k) contributions except that: (a) the rule applies on a plan-by-plan basis; and (b) in the event of a roll-in, the predecessor plan's history is applied. Generally and very importantly, if amounts are distributed from a Roth IRA and the distribution is not a qualified distribution, they are first sourced tax-free from "basis" (i.e. amounts that were converted or Roth IRA contributions), and thereafter are sourced from (taxable) earnings.

Roth IRA Strategies. Special planning options exist for Roth IRAs. An individual can have an unlimited number of traditional IRAs and Roth IRAs.

Having some Roth assets produces tax diversification. And, diversification reduces risk. Having Roth money during retirement would permit a retiree to time Roth distributions and traditional IRA distributions, such that a relatively larger dose of traditional IRA distributions could be taken in years when significant deductions exist, such as medical deductions. Having some Roth accounts permits a blend of Roth and traditional IRA distributions to avoid or minimize income taxes in retirement.

Many seniors are in a low or no income tax bracket. If they make a Roth conversion, the cost will be little or nothing. However, upon death, the tax-free benefits to children or grandchildren (or nieces, nephews, grandnieces or grandnephews) could be very substantial.

Some other more complex strategies exist, such as borrowing money from a Roth account in a 401(k) plan to leverage the account and make more tax-free income. However, as explained below, debt-financing produces income tax consequences.

Contribution Limits. Under Code section 4973, a six percent (6%) excise tax potentially applies to a nondeductible contribution to an IRA. Under Code §408(a)(1), with the exception of a rollover contribution, only cash can be contributed to an IRA. While property can be contributed to a tax-qualified plan, a transfer of encumbered property (i.e. property subject to a liability) to a tax-qualified pension plan is a prohibited transaction. (Prohibited transactions are discussed below.) The performance of services by the IRA owner for the IRA could possibly be an excessive contribution or a prohibited transaction (or both).

In recent years, many individuals have turned to their IRAs to purchase real estate and other non-publicly traded investments. Often, this is done because personal financing cannot be obtained. Sometimes, the objective is to form or acquire a business.

There are approximately ten (10) significant companies that will serve as custodian for non-publicly-traded assets of IRAs. (The large IRA companies will not do so.) These companies typically require full indemnification for prohibited transactions exposure. They charge annual fees as well as fees to handle transactions. If an active business or rental activity will exist, it may be best to form an LLC to operate the business, so as to reduce the incidence of fee charges by the custodian.

Other Considerations

New QBI Deduction. Some professional tax and pension advisors have been advising that tax-qualified plan contributions (and tax-qualified plans) are now a "loser," given the new QBI deduction. The truth is otherwise.

Consider the FAFSA example from the end of Chapter 7, wherein a 52-year old lawyer who is part of a family of four makes $200,000 from a law practice. The family's tax return included a $25,000 401(k) contribution, HDHP contributions of $1,200 per month and an HSA contribution of $7,900. Consider if the attorney "maxed out" on his 401(k)/profit sharing plan (instead of doing either of the options presented in that example), thus producing an additional $37,000 of deductible contributions. If the year is 2019 and Georgia's tax system applies, the net federal and state tax/health care savings would be $7,201. The $37,000 deduction reduced the QBI deduction by $7,400 (i.e. 37,000 x .2). The tax rate benefit is 19.5 percent (i.e. 7,201/37,000). For 2019, the federal rate for a joint return with taxable income between $19,400 and $78,950 is 12 percent. It is very likely that the federal incremental tax rate for the couple would fall within this range, if current law applied (adjusted for inflation) when they later retired. Georgia has a large exemption for seniors. Assuming a 3 percent state rate and 12 percent federal rate applies during retirement, the after-tax difference is supplied in the following chart.

Receive cash:		Defer to 401(k):			
Initial Amount:	29799	Initial Amount:	37000		
6% earnings, net of 28% tax	1287	Growth:	2220		
Total after year 1	31086	Total after year 1	39220		
6% earnings, net of 28% tax	1343	Growth:	2353		
Total after year 2	32429	Total after year 2	41573		
6% earnings, net of 28% tax	1401	Growth:	2494		
Total after year 3	33830	Total after year 3	44068		
6% earnings, net of 28% tax	1461	Growth:	2644		
Total after year 4	35292	Total after year 4	46712		
6% earnings, net of 28% tax	1525	Growth:	2803		
Total after year 5	36816	Total after year 5	49514	x .85	42087
6% earnings, net of 28% tax	1590	Growth:	2971		
Total after year 6	38407	Total after year 6	52485		
6% earnings, net of 28% tax	1659	Growth:	3149		
Total after year 7	40066	Total after year 7	55634		
6% earnings, net of 28% tax	1731	Growth:	3338		
Total after year 8	41797	Total after year 8	58972		
6% earnings, net of 28% tax	1806	Growth:	3538		
Total after year 9	43602	Total after year 9	62511		
6% earnings, net of 28% tax	1884	Growth:	3751		
Total after year 10	45486	Total after year 10	66261	x .85	56322
6% earnings, net of 28% tax	1965	Growth:	3976		
Total after year 11	47451	Total after year 11	70237		
6% earnings, net of 28% tax	2050	Growth:	4214		
Total after year 12	49501	Total after year 12	74451		
6% earnings, net of 28% tax	2138	Growth:	4467		
Total after year 13	51639	Total after year 13	78918		
6% earnings, net of 28% tax	2231	Growth:	4735		
Total after year 14	53870	Total after year 14	83653		
6% earnings, net of 28% tax	2327	Growth:	5019		
Total after year 15	56197	Total after year 15	88673	x .85	75372

The assumed net federal/state percent rate under the first column above is 28. The longer the deferral, the greater is the benefit. Making the contribution makes financial sense. Of course, it always makes sense to "run the numbers."

Some professional tax and pension advisors are recommending making Roth contributions (which, as noted, have their limits) in lieu of making traditional 401(k) contributions. As the following changes from the above example show, converting the traditional 401(k) contribution makes little difference. The tax savings of the traditional 401(k) contribution (again, using Georgia law) is $4,369.

Receive cash:		Defer to 401(k):		Defer to Roth 401(k):	
Initital Amount:	4369	Initial Amount:	25000	Initial Amount:	25000
6% earnings, net of 28% tax	189	Growth:	1500	Growth:	1500
Total after year 1	4558	Total after year 1	26500	Total after year 1	26500
6% earnings, net of 28% tax	197	Growth:	1590	Growth:	1590
Total after year 2	4755	Total after year 2	28090	Total after year 2	28090
6% earnings, net of 28% tax	205	Growth:	1685	Growth:	1685
Total after year 3	4960	Total after year 3	29775	Total after year 3	29775
6% earnings, net of 28% tax	214	Growth:	1787	Growth:	1787
Total after year 4	5174	Total after year 4	31562	Total after year 4	31562
6% earnings, net of 28% tax	224	Growth:	1894	Growth:	1894
Total after year 5	5398	Total after year 5	33456 x .85 28437	Total after year 5	33456
6% earnings, net of 28% tax	233	Growth:	2007	Growth:	2007
Total after year 6	5631	Total after year 6	35463	Total after year 6	35463
6% earnings, net of 28% tax	243	Growth:	2128	Growth:	2128
Total after year 7	5874	Total after year 7	37591	Total after year 7	37591
6% earnings, net of 28% tax	254	Growth:	2255	Growth:	2255
Total after year 8	6128	Total after year 8	39846	Total after year 8	39846
6% earnings, net of 28% tax	265	Growth:	2391	Growth:	2391
Total after year 9	6393	Total after year 9	42237	Total after year 9	42237
6% earnings, net of 28% tax	276	Growth:	2534	Growth:	2534
Total after year 10	6669	Total after year 10	44771 x .85 38056	Total after year 10	44771
6% earnings, net of 28% tax	288	Growth:	2686	Growth:	2686
Total after year 11	6957	Total after year 11	47457	Total after year 11	47457
6% earnings, net of 28% tax	301	Growth:	2847	Growth:	2847

Total after year 12	7258	Total after year 12	50305		Total after year 12	50305
Total after year 12	7258	Total after year 12	50305		Total after year 12	50305
6% earnings, net of 28% tax	314	Growth:	3018		Growth:	3018
Total after year 13	7571	Total after year 13	53323		Total after year 13	53323
6% earnings, net of 28% tax	327	Growth:	3199		Growth:	3199
Total after year 14	7898	Total after year 14	56523		Total after year 14	56523
6% earnings, net of 28% tax	341	Growth:	3391		Growth:	3391
Total after year 15	8239	Total after year 15	59914 x .85 50927	Total after year 15	59914
Sum of Traditional Benefits at year 15:			59166	Roth benefits:	59914

It should be noted that the above examples didn't produce any ACA benefits. If a cash balance plan had been used in the first example above (where $62,000 was contributed to a tax-qualified plan) and $8,000 additional was contributed to it (for a total of $70,000) or $8,000 of deductible IRA contributions were made by the taxpayer and spouse in addition to the $62,000 contributed to the 401(k)/profit sharing plan, then the combined tax/health care savings would increase by $14,400. Almost all of the additional benefits are ACA benefits.

UBTI. Both a tax-qualified plan and an IRA are potentially subject to the unrelated business income tax ("UBIT") of Code section 511. Under section 511, the unrelated business taxable income ("UBTI") of a tax-qualified plan or an IRA is taxed in a manner similar to the manner in which an individual is taxed, except that the plan or IRA is treated as a trust (meaning the highest bracket is reached very quickly). TJCA slightly modified how UBTI is calculated, so as to make UBTI liability slightly more likely.

Generally, UBTI is income from a commercial business (e.g. a restaurant) that is regularly carried on. However, exceptions exist, including an important exception for real estate. However, the exceptions are subject to the debt financing exception of Code section 514, such that debt-financed real estate income of an IRA is UBTI. A limited real estate exception exists for tax-qualified plans. So, if a tax-qualified plan or an IRA borrowed funds and used the funds to purchase an interest in a business venture, ordinarily the income would be UBTI.

Prohibited Transactions. Under Code section 4975, a prohibited transaction gives rise to a 15 percent excise tax on the amount involved. The tax rate is increased to 100 percent if correction does not occur within a statutory time frame. If a third party fiduciary commits a prohibited transaction, it must pay the tax. However, if the IRA owner or beneficiary of an IRA commits a prohibited transaction, the excise taxes do not apply. Instead, the IRA ceases to be an IRA on the first day of the year in which the prohibited transaction occurs, and the assets are deemed to have been distributed on such day. The result is the full value of the IRA is taxable, except to the extent of any non-deductible contributions previously made. Thereafter, the assets are deemed owned outright by the individual.

A prohibited transaction is defined as one of certain transactions between or involving a "plan" and a "disqualified person." The term "plan" includes a tax-qualified plan and an IRA. A disqualified person includes a fiduciary with respect to a tax-qualified plan or IRA and a person providing services to the plan or IRA. Family members of disqualified persons, excluding siblings, cousins, aunts, and uncles, are also disqualified persons. Also included in the definition are corporations and partnerships (including LLCs) of which or in which the fiduciary or service provider directly or indirectly owns 50 percent or more of the combined voting power of all classes of stock entitled to vote or the total value of all classes of stock of the corporation or, with respect to a partnership (or LLC), 50 percent or more of the capital interests or profits interests. An officer, director, highly compensated employee or ten percent or greater owner of such an entity also is a disqualified person. An employer of an employee who is a plan participant is a disqualified person with respect to the employee's plan account. (It's unclear how this rule works with an IRA.)

While a disqualified person is very specifically statutorily defined, the term "plan" is not well defined, except for a listing of plan types (e.g. tax-qualified, IRA, etc.) that qualify. This lack of a solid definition for what a plan "is" (to quote Bill Clinton) makes application of the prohibited transaction rules very difficult. If an IRA simply owns cash, then a use of such cash to buy something from a disqualified person would, absent an exemption, be a prohibited transaction. The same would be true of most other assets owned by the plan (or IRA). But, when the plan or IRA owns an interest in a legal entity, things get dicey. In this regard, people who work in the tax field are used to "looking through" entities for direct and indirect ownership of what the entity owns. But, given the very specific attribution rules, the very specific definition of a disqualified person and the lack of the same for a plan, arguably, the definition goes no further than assets directly owned. Further, the plan asset rules (discussed below) pick up indirectly owned entities, subject to the significant exceptions thereto.

Subject to exemptions, under subsection (c)(1) of Code section 4975, prohibited transactions include any direct or indirect:

(A) a sale or exchange, or leasing, of any property between a plan and a disqualified person;

(B) lending of money or other extension of credit between a plan and a disqualified person;

(C) furnishing of goods, services or facilities between a plan and a disqualified person;

(D) transfer to, or use for the benefit of, a disqualified person of the income or assets of a plan (so, personal use is prohibited);

(E) act by a disqualified person who is a fiduciary whereby he deals with the income or assets of the plan in his own interests or for his own account; or

(F) receipt of any consideration for his own personal account by a disqualified person who is a fiduciary from any party dealing with the plan in connection with a transaction involving the income or assets of the plan.

Exceptions exist in the form of exemptions, including an exemption relating to any benefit a person is entitled to as a plan beneficiary (e.g. investment returns—subsection (d)(9)) and receipt of reasonable compensation by a disqualified person for services rendered in performance of his "duties with the plan" (subsection (d)(10)). However, under the (d)(10) exemption, if a disqualified person is already receiving full-time pay from a company that participates in or sponsors the plan, he cannot receive additional compensation for services relating to the plan. Also, under subsection (d)(2), reasonable compensation can be provided under a contract or arrangement for office, legal, accounting or other services necessary for the establishment or operation of the plan. It appears that these provisions were meant to apply exclusively to plan-related services, and not to any other services. However, the authorities discussing them, including IRS materials, suggest a greater scope potentially exists.

A fiduciary is defined as a person who: (A) exercises any discretionary authority or discretionary control respecting management of a plan or exercises any authority or control respecting management or disposition of the plan's assets; (B) renders investment advice for a fee or other compensation, direct or indirect, with respect to any moneys or other property of such plan, or has any authority or responsibility to do so; or (C) has any discretionary authority or discretionary responsibility in the administration of such plan. The IRA owner of a self-directed IRA is a fiduciary (and a disqualified person). A custodian may take the position that it is not a disqualified person.

Treasury Regulation section 54.4975-6(a)(5)(i) and (ii) provide the following guidance on prohibited activities by fiduciaries:

> (ii) . . . Thus, a fiduciary may not use the authority, control, or responsibility which makes such person a fiduciary to cause a plan to pay an additional fee to such fiduciary (or to a person in which such fiduciary has an interest which may affect the exercise of such fiduciary's best judgment as a fiduciary) to provide a service. Nor may a fiduciary use such authority, control, or responsibility to cause a plan to enter into a transaction involving plan assets whereby such fiduciary (or a person in which such fiduciary has an interest which may affect the exercise of such fiduciary's best judgment as a fiduciary) will receive compensation from a third party in connection with such transaction. . . .

Some case law (but not much) exists with respect to prohibited transactions. One case holds that the guarantee of a loan to a disqualified person by the IRA's owner is a prohibited transaction. There are not many other prohibited transactions authorities. So, this area is very difficult to work in, particularly if certainty is sought. *Some things may not add up*—some court decisions may not make sense. The statute is not a model of clarity.

If there is a concern that a transaction desired to be undertaken with respect to an IRA will be a prohibited transaction, it would be best to transfer (roll over) the assets to be involved in the transaction to a separate IRA before undertaking the transaction. IRAs are not aggregated when a prohibited transaction analysis is undertaken, meaning a disqualification of an IRA due to a prohibited transaction will have no bearing on any other IRAs. Obviously, less flexibility exists with respect to a tax-qualified plan since, unlike an IRA, a tax-qualified plan cannot be established on a whim at little or no cost.

Plan Asset Rules. With respect to nonpublicly-traded equity interests (in any entity), the plan asset rules generally require *both* the entity investment and the entity's assets, to the extent of proportionate ownership, to be deemed owned by the IRA (or retirement plan) for purposes of the fiduciary duty and prohibited transaction rules. For example, the assets of an LLC wholly-owned by an IRA would be deemed to be owned by the IRA. A single member LLC is a disregarded entity for federal tax purposes, meaning that the assets would be taken into account, but not the LLC interest, for purposes of Code section 4975. When the plan asset rules apply, persons with the ability to exercise authority or control of the management or disposition of the underlying plan assets are deemed to be fiduciaries with respect to the owning IRA.

Some important exceptions exist to the plan asset rules, including an exception for operating companies and a statutory exception that applies if benefit plan investors (including tax-qualified plans and IRAs) own less than 25 percent of each class of equity interest of the entity. An operating company generally is a company that is primarily engaged in the production or sale of a product or service other than investment of capital. Also included in the definition of an operating company is a real estate operating company, which generally means a company engaged in the management or development of real estate, at least 50 percent of the costs of the assets of which is real estate that is managed or developed by the company. An exception also exists for certain venture capital operating companies. However, none of these exceptions applies if the IRA holds all of the equity interests.

Section 409A Considerations. Internal Revenue Code section 409A was enacted in 2004 generally to prevent executives from being able to push back or accelerate a benefit under a retirement plan other than a tax-qualified plan. Basically, Code section 409A applies to any compensation that is earned today (and to which legal entitlement to payment exists) but is paid in a future year. If there is a section 409A violation (for failure to pay pursuant to plan terms at the time specified when the benefits were earned), the employee is the one who incurs the tax. The tax is income inclusion of all amounts not subject to a substantial risk of forfeiture[6] when first not subject to a substantial risk of forfeiture, plus interest and a 20 percent penalty.

Generally, tax-qualified plan and IRA benefits are exempt from section 409A. Also exempt are incentive stock options (ISOs), nonqualified options and stock appreciation rights, as long as the option price for the stock is fair market value or greater on the date of grant. An important exception to section 409A exists for bonuses paid within 2½ months after the end of the employer's or the employee's taxable year. Other exceptions exist, including a severance

---

[6] Compensation is subject to a substantial risk of forfeiture if entitlement to the amount is conditioned on the performance of substantial future services by any person or the occurrence of a condition related to purpose of the compensation, and the possibility of forfeiture is substantial.

pay exception. If a deferred compensation plan specifies in the plan or agreement exactly when compensation earned today will be paid in the future, and it is followed, then compliance ordinarily would exist.

Target Date Funds. Most employees can invest in 401(k) plans. Many employees are not knowledgeable about investments. Combined, these facts led to the creation of "target date" funds. Target date funds have a date attached to them, which is designed to correspond to a participant's retirement date. For example, a "2034 fund" would be pitched to a plan participant who is age 50 in 2019 if the plan's normal retirement age is 65 (as is often the case). Target date funds with a distant retirement date (e.g. 40 years into the future) start heavily invested in stocks and other more aggressive investments and lightly invested in bonds and other more conservative investments, and gradually become less invested in stocks and more aggressive investments and more invested in bonds and other less aggressive investments. For example, in 2019, a 2050 fund might be invested 80 percent in stocks and 20 percent in bonds, while the 2020 fund might be invested 20 percent in stocks and 80 percent in bonds and more traditionally conservative investments. (In 2045, the 2050 fund might be invested 75 percent in bonds and other traditionally conservative investments and 25 percent in stocks.)

There are "to" and "through" target date funds. A "to" fund targets the normal retirement age as its ending point. A "through" fund targets the anticipated end of life as its ending point (applying life expectancy), under the assumption that following normal retirement age the participant will continue to invest in stocks, bonds and other investments through either the plan or an IRA. So, a "through" fund would ordinarily have a higher investment percentage in stocks than a "to" fund at any given time, including at normal retirement age.

Historically, bonds have been considered to be less risky than stocks. Thus, the gradual move to more conservative investments (mainly bonds) as one gets closer to retirement age makes sense if bonds truly are less risky than stocks. However, interest rates have been near historic lows in recent years. And, when interest rates increase, bond values decrease. Some believe interest rates will increase substantially in the next several years. In January 2019, the Congressional Budget Office (CBO) predicted the 10-year Treasury note rate would increase from 3.0 percent in the 4th quarter of 2018 to 3.8 percent in 2022. (It was 2.1 percent in the 4th quarter of 2016.) If rates go up substantially and bond values fall substantially, many near term (e.g. 2025) target date funds that are heavily invested in long-term bonds will very likely experience value losses. Many plan fiduciaries are aware of this potential problem, and are taking actions to reduce the potential for loss such as by using a higher concentration of short-term bonds instead of long-term bonds (because the shorter a bond's term, the lesser its value will be detrimentally impacted by interest rate increases). Investment in Treasury Inflation Protected Securities is now common for a significant part of the conservative portion of the portfolio.

ESOPs. As explained in Chapter 5, employee stock ownership plans (ESOPs) can provide tremendous tax benefits, including tax-free sales of company stock to the ESOP. Generally, under Code section 1042, at least 30 percent of the company's stock must be owned by the ESOP following the sale in order for the sale to be tax-free. For tax-free treatment to apply, only certain types of investments can be purchased with the proceeds. The investments' adjusted basis in the investments purchased with the sales proceeds is reduced by the amount of gain not recognized on the sale of the company stock. Ordinarily, the stock purchase is financed by a third party, and paid for over a period of years (e.g. ten years). As the loan is repaid, stock is allocated to participants' ESOP accounts, causing them to be the indirect owners of the company. If the corporation is a C corporation and an S election is made following the sale, the ESOP's annual share of company profit is not subject to income tax. Also, the ESOP of an S corporation can provide for only cash distributions. ESOPs are often undertaken when the owner or owners of a company wish to sell the company and have not found a suitable buyer. ERISA's fiduciary duties apply to the sale and the ESOP, making these transactions potentially risky. If the facts are right, because of the tremendous tax benefits, an ESOP can be a great thing.

Chapter 9

Non-Saving Preparation for Retirement

Social Security Benefits. Social Security is a legally required retirement plan for those who work. Benefits are calculated by indexing earnings for wage inflation prior to age 60, taking the average of the highest 35 years, dividing by twelve to produce average indexed monthly earnings (AIME), and then applying a progressive benefit formula to AIME. For those eligible to retire in 2019, the formula is 90 percent of the first $926 of AIME, 32 percent of the next $4,557 of AIME and 15 percent of any AIME in excess of $5,583. So, for example, if someone retired at normal retirement age in 2019 with AIME of $4,000, their single life annuity benefit would be $1,817, equal to (($926 x .9) + ((4,000-926) x .32)).

The ordinary benefit is reduced for early retirement. The reduction is 5/9ths of one percent for the first 36 months preceding full retirement age, and 5/12ths of one percent for months prior thereto. For example, a person born in 1952 would have a full (or normal) retirement age of 66, and would experience a 25 percent reduction if benefits commenced at the earliest retirement age (62). The ordinary benefit is increased by 2/3rds of one percent per month that a benefit begins after full retirement age, up until age 70 (where increases cease).

Cost of living adjustments (COLAs) are ordinarily given to Social Security beneficiaries. However, in recent years, COLAs have not always been given. COLAs are tied to inflation.

The full retirement age has been gradually increasing from 65 to 67. People born in 1960 and thereafter have an age 67 full retirement age. Social Security benefits increase by roughly 8 percent per year that benefits are deferred beyond full retirement age, until age 70. Thus, for those who believe they'll outlive normal life expectancy, waiting to take benefits at age 70 could be beneficial. The system's solvency needs to be considered.

If all Social Security benefits will be paid (which is uncertain), life expectancy dictates when is best to begin receiving benefits. Timing strategies exist for married couples. Various websites provide guidance. See, for example, these websites: SocialSecurityChoices.com, SocialSecuritySolutions.com and MaximizeMySocialSecurity.com. Social Security can be reached at (800) 772-1213, and its website is www.ssa.gov.

Recent articles about Social Security show that uncertainty in the security of Social Security system makes planning next to impossible. Under current law, benefits are scheduled to continue to 2034 (when the "trust fund" will be exhausted), and thereafter be cut by approximately 23 percent. However, the trust fund is merely comprised of Treasury bill (IOUs) from the federal government (which has few liquid assets).

A May 2015 *Money* magazine article stated that, generally, a single beneficiary breaks even on taking Social Security benefits early (at age 62) if he or she lives to (but not beyond) age 80½. The article presumably assumed benefits will not be cut in the future. It also noted that a 65 year old has a 49 chance of living to age 85 or older. Life expectancy can be calculated using the Actuaries Longevity Illustrator. (It can be found via internet search.)

QLACs. In 2014, the IRS issued final regulations permitting participants in defined contributions plans such as 401(k) plans and traditional IRAs to purchase longevity annuities. Basically, a longevity annuity begins payment of an annuity at a particular age, not to exceed 85. The regulations relate to Internal Revenue Code §401(a)(9)'s minimum required distribution (MRD) requirements. The rules do not apply to Roth IRAs (because the MRD rules do not apply to Roth IRAs). For 2019, applicable regulations generally limit the amount of an account balance that can be used to purchase a Qualifying Longevity Annuity Contract (QLAC) to the lesser of 25 percent of the account balance or $130,000. Requirements exist in order for an annuity to quality as a QLAC, but a QLAC can permit a refund of the premium(s) paid to the extent they exceed benefits paid. The section 401(a)(9) benefit of a QLAC is that the investment is excluded from the account balance for purposes of MRD calculations. Thus, it reduces pre-annuity start MRDs. For 401(k) plans, there is a fiduciary obligation to permit only prudent investments with respect to plan assets. Therefore, fiduciaries will need to evaluate potential insurer options for creditworthiness. An IRA could purchase a life annuity that is not a QLAC. However, the annuity's value would need to be included when calculating MRDs.

An April 16, 2015 article by actuary Ken Steiner analyzed the prudence of taking Social Security at Social Security normal retirement age (instead of deferring until age 70), and purchasing a QLAC funded from an IRA or qualified plan's assets with assets that otherwise would have been distributed from an IRA for subsistence. Based on an analysis using certain currently reasonable assumptions, assuming Social Security benefits will never be cut, Mr. Steiner concluded that using the retirement savings that would have been distributed and expended to make it to age 70 to buy a $52,000 deferred annuity beginning at age 85 makes more sense than not buying such an annuity and waiting until age 70 to begin receiving

Social Security benefits. Then, Mr. Steiner noted the anticipated 23 percent shortfall in 2034 changes the analysis (making not deferring Social Security benefits even more appealing). He also noted that interest rates will likely increase and more companies will begin selling QLACs, with the likely result being reduced costs for QLACs. He did not make a final recommendation.

Most QLACs will provide for a return of principal. However, if a QLAC is purchased 15 or more years before the first anticipated payment will be made, the present value of future payments will likely be less than the outlay for the policy if the purchaser will experience a normal life expectancy or live less than a normal life expectancy. The insurance company that offers the policy will have priced it to make money. Generally, only if the purchaser outlives normal life expectancy can a QLAC potentially be a profitable asset.

To the extent one believes Social Security is a sure thing, it might be best to consider looking at Social Security as a fixed income, defined benefit type source of income with inflation protection. Doing so might prompt a person to take a different outlook with respect to the retirement portfolio he/she controls. In other words, if someone wants a certain amount of fixed (i.e. supposedly guaranteed) income and a certain amount of market return, Social Security benefits could be considered part of the fixed income portfolio.

Anticipating Incapacity; Nursing Home Care. Nursing home costs account for roughly half of all federal Medicaid costs. Although Medicaid is a joint federal/state program, in every state, the federal government funds at least half the costs. Medicaid pays approximately forty percent (40%) of long-term nursing care costs in the U.S. The U.S. Code provides certain overriding requirements that states must follow to receive funding. Otherwise, state law and regulations supply the applicable rules. In many states, nursing homes have significant political muscle, and they negotiate significant rates.

Nursing home costs vary significantly by state and by area within a state. For a private room in Georgia in 2018, the average monthly cost was $6,768. Also in Georgia in 2018, monthly costs for a semi-private room averaged $6,342. Medicaid provides for only a semi-private room. For an ordinary person, nursing home costs can wipe out a tremendous amount of wealth, given that the average stay is several years.

To be eligible for nursing home Medicaid benefits from a medical perspective, ordinarily, a person must be in need of an "Intermediate Level of Care." To have an Intermediate Level of Care need *generally* means the person cannot take care of himself or herself. (A very specific set of criteria must be met.) In Georgia, generally, a nursing home administrator must sign a form stating that the person meets the intermediate care standard. Also in Georgia, a person must be age 65 or older or blind or disabled to be eligible. A beneficiary must agree to assign his or her right to all forms of income to the State of Georgia for state funding to apply. A 30-day nursing home stay is required in Georgia in order for benefits to be available.

While some entitlements (e.g. ACA premiums assistance) focus exclusively on income, in order to be eligible for free or subsidized nursing home care, an asset test and an income test must be passed. These tests place limits on assets that can be owned and income that can be received.

Generally, with an important large exemption for home equity, no more than $2,000 of "countable" assets can be owned by a single person. The single person home equity exemption for 2019 in Georgia is $585,000. For married persons, the combined asset limit for 2019 is $128,420 and there is no limit on home equity. (Note: A spouse can petition to have the $128,420 limit increased.) For purposes of the asset test, generally, assets owned by both spouses are taken into account. Other exemptions and exceptions apply, including household goods and personal effects, one vehicle used for transportation (which could be a wheelchair accessible van), and certain property used in a trade or business that is needed for self-support. A married beneficiary must transfer assets in excess of $2,000 to his or her spouse within one year of eligibility in order to remain eligible. A financial power of attorney can be very helpful in this regard.

State law determines the income limit. In Georgia, the limit is three times the Supplemental Security Income (SSI) annual figure. For 2019, the SSI figure is $771, meaning a Georgia person could have up to $2,313 of income and potentially qualify for Medicaid nursing home coverage. However, in Georgia, a much greater amount of income can exist if a Medicaid Qualified Income Trust (a "Miller" trust) is used. Miller trusts are common in certain states, such as Georgia. In other states, different rules apply. In many states, if income does not exceed the nursing home charges and other requirements are met, the income requirement is deemed met.

Only the income of the Medicaid beneficiary is considered for eligibility purposes. "Income" means economic income, not taxable income. Certain forms of income are exempt, including loan proceeds, the value of a personal service, Veteran's Aid & Attendance and Veteran's Unreimbursed Medical Expense.

A Miller Trust collects all of the beneficiary's income and then pays out the income for certain permissible uses, including a personal allowance, a generous allowance for a spouse, a generous allowance for dependent children, health insurance coverage and the beneficiary's share of the cost of nursing home care. In Georgia in 2019, the beneficiary's monthly share of the cost of nursing home care is the excess of the month's income over the sum of a $65 personal allowance (a greater amount for certain veterans), a payment to the spouse sufficient to increase his or her income to the amount needed to survive up to $3,160.50, a payment to each dependent family member living in the home other than the spouse necessary to increase his or her income to $2,313, payment of health insurance premiums and payment of non-Medicaid covered health care expenses. (Notes: The $3,160.50 is the Minimum Monthly Needs Allowance (MMNA). A spouse can petition to have the $3,160.50 figure increased if the amount will not cover his/her needs.)

42 U.S.C. §1396p is the federal statute that specifies federal financial requirements for eligibility and certain other things. Generally, all assets transferred more than five years prior to nursing home entry are not considered in determining whether the asset test is met. (Under subsection (c)(1)(B), a five-year look back period applies to Medicaid applicants.) Generally, if a state resident transfers all of his or her wealth at least five years prior to applying for Medicaid, and has net countable assets of $2,000 or less when applying, the person can qualify for Medicaid coverage of nursing home care if the income test is met and the person is in need of nursing home care. Gifts and asset transfers for less than fair market value within the five year

period by the applicant or his/her spouse reduce potential benefits by requiring the person to pay for coverage for the number of months equal to the net amounts transferred within the five year period divided by the average monthly cost for nursing home care in the state. Hardship exceptions exist to the 5-year rule.

Exceptions to the five-year lookback transfer rule apply to payment of a valid debt, payment to a spouse, transfer of a home to a sibling who has an equity interest in the home and has lived in the home for at least one year, and transfer to a child who has lived in the home for at least two years if the child's services have prevented the beneficiary from needing to be placed in a nursing home. An exception exists for a payment to a statutory special needs trust. Generally, funds can be paid to a relative to provide care, room and/or board. As long as the payments are reasonable and certain requirements are met (including there being a written contract and care *actually being provided* on arm's length terms), they are considered legitimate expenses and are not considered transfers for less than fair market value for purposes of the lookback rule. The service provider will need to recognize income for payments received, and FICA tax withholding might be required by the payer. Some states permit a lump-sum payment to cover future services.

Retirement accounts and IRAs (but not pension plan accrued benefits) are countable assets. Like virtually all of the rules relating to nursing home care, state-specific rules apply to retirement assets. In Georgia, a person age 70½ or greater generally can avoid inclusion by receiving MRDs under Code §401(a)(9) (and such distributions are necessary to avoid excise taxes). Purchasing a life annuity could be a means of dealing with retirement accounts. Retirement accounts of the spouse are not considered (i.e.

are exempt). The assets held in a statutory special needs trust are not countable assets.

Annuities purchased with assets held outside a retirement plan that are non-assignable, actuarially sound and provide equal payments with no deferral or balloon generally are exempt from the asset list, and the purchase of such an annuity does not constitute an assets disposal for less than fair market value. (Income from the annuity would count as income for purposes of the income test.) Similarly, payment of assets for a promissory note may not be deemed a transfer for less than fair market value and the note exempt, provided it has features similar to those of an annuity. A purchase by a spouse often is a big help, as his or her income is not countable for eligibility purposes. These type assets are particularly complex and, like other areas discussed herein, justify retention of a professional advisor.

Certain prepaid burial expenses are exempt and do not trigger the lookback, including payment for a cemetery plot or grave site. In Georgia, a $10,000 exemption can be applied to other prepaid expenses relating to death (that are not exempt). In Georgia, life insurance with a face value in excess of $10,000 is a countable asset. For whole life insurance, the cash surrender value is counted.

Concerning "spend down" planning (to reduce assets), a home can be expanded or refurbished. Also, a debt can be paid. If a "solid" family relationship exists, assets can be transferred to a child or children five or more years prior to the potential need for nursing home care (to the extent such can be determined). When making any asset transfers, the basis "step up" rule of Internal Revenue Code should be kept in mind. In this regard, assets owned by a decedent receive a step-up (or step-down) to fair market value at death. (A grantor trust can cause assets to be deemed owned by the grantor.) In some states, retirement plan accounts can be annuitized, and annuities can be purchased with non-retirement assets. Certain post-death expenses can be prepaid. Other possibilities exist.

State recovery exists following the death of the Medicaid beneficiary or, in many cases, following the death of the beneficiary's spouse. Under state recovery, assets can be taken to reimburse the state the out-of-pocket costs it incurred on behalf of the beneficiary. In Georgia, the home is not exempt unless the estate is valued at $25,000 or less. If a spouse continues to live in the home, the home is exempt until the earlier of the spouse's death or the sale of the home. In Georgia, interest is not charged with respect to estate recovery. Georgia allows a $25,000 home equity allowance for survivors/heirs.

Regarding estate recovery, Georgia tends to go after more than the probate estate of a beneficiary (following death). For example, Georgia has had a history of pursuing real estate owned jointly with the right of survivorship, as well as retirement assets such as IRA benefits. However, the applicable federal law as applied in Georgia very likely limits estate recovery to probate assets. State law can be extended to cover real estate and other assets passing by deeds, but unless an IRA or retirement benefit qualifies as personal property, such benefits should be exempt from recovery under the laws of every state.

If someone who is disabled is receiving public benefits, receipt of a bequest can cause them to be ineligible for public benefits. For example, in Georgia, if a single person owns more than $2,000 in assets he/she is ineligible for Medicaid (including nursing home care). Thus, care should be taken in estate planning documents to make sure that a person who is disabled, or may become disabled in the future (i.e. anyone) will not receive an outright bequest if the bequest would disqualify the person from public benefits. Instead, the bequest should be paid to a special needs trust, etc. so that benefits will continue uninterrupted.

Assisted Living and Other Types of Living Arrangements. Outside nursing home care, other forms of help exist for people who don't have an Intermediate Level of Care need. Perhaps most common is assisted living. In Georgia in 2018, the average monthly cost was $3,100.

Assisted living offers less help to the elderly and disabled than does a nursing home. Ordinarily, subject to state-specific rules, there is no requirement that a licensed nurse be on premises at an assisted living facility. And, the degree to which public benefits are available to help fund the cost varies by state. For example, Georgia does not provide public benefits to help fund assisted living. However, Georgia still regulates assisted living providers that operate in Georgia.

Other care options exist, including a personal care home, where elderly and disabled persons live in a residential setting (typically a home). The states can regulate these arrangements as well. In-home care also exists, where home caregivers that are usually hired by an agency come to the elderly or disabled person's home and provide services. Adult day care also is an option, whereby the senior or disabled person spends the day at a facility that provides social, nutritional and other support services. In Georgia, Medicaid benefits are not available for these options. The funding source for these options ordinarily is long-term insurance, VA pension benefits or private funds.

For those with substantial savings and anticipated significant income in retirement, a Continuing Care

Retirement Community (CCRC) can be appealing. Generally, a life estate is purchased in a residential unit by paying the value of the unit upfront. Significant monthly fees apply. Medical care and numerous amenities, groups and clubs exist. Following death of the tenant (or the last to die if a couple), the initial investment is repaid (or is transferrable to heirs).

A reverse mortgage can be a worthwhile option for those who have lived in their home awhile and have built up substantial equity. (The technical name for a reverse mortgage is a Home Equity Conversion Mortgage (HECM).) A loan is made based on the equity in the home. The loan does not require monthly payments, but interest charges increase the loan balance. Upon death of the owner or a move, the loan is due. Federal law limits how much can be loaned. High closing costs often apply.

Long-Term Care Insurance. Long-term care insurance is growing in popularity. As of the end of 2016, roughly ten percent of Americans had purchased such coverage. Most policies sold are now hybrid life insurance policies, so that a certain minimum return is produced by the policy. Significant medical underwriting is generally required before coverage will be issued. Policies typically place limits on the time benefits will be paid (e.g. 3 years) and the total amount of benefits that will be paid either daily or in total. Depending on policy terms, benefits can be provided for nursing home care, assisted living, in-home care and adult day care. The tough call here is whether it is better to go this route or forego coverage and essentially self-insure.

For income tax purposes, subject to limits that increase with age, premiums on long-term care insurance paid by persons other than self-employed persons are treated as medical expenses. Total medical expenses are deductible as itemized deductions to the extent they exceed ten percent of AGI. Self-employed persons, including partners (and most LLC members) and two-percent or greater S shareholders can, subject to the limits that change by age, deduct premiums. The age limits are specified in Code section 213(d). They are listed in Chapter 5.

Like the federal government, most states are experiencing significant financial pressure. Many of them have drastically underfunded pension and other post-retirement benefit (mainly health care) plans. So, the caveats noted in the first chapter about future practices and laws changing substantially apply equally to the states.

Chapter 10

Anticipating Disability & Providing for the Disabled

Insurance. Disability insurance can be purchased to reduce exposure to risk of loss of income while working. Social Security also provides for disability benefits. However, its "trust fund" is not exactly flush with assets. Long-term care insurance is becoming more commonplace, although some considerations make purchasing it undesirable, particularly in certain states.

Special Needs Trusts. A special needs trust is a trust set up under state law that meets the requirements of 42 U.S.C. §1396p(d)(4). So, a special needs trust falls within the same federal regulatory scope as nursing home care.

Amounts contributed to an ordinary trust by an individual for his benefit are considered a resource for Medicaid purposes. Similarly, assets held by a person in a revocable trust are considered a (potentially disqualifying) resource. Any interest a person holds in an irrevocable trust, including the possibility of receiving the benefits of assets of an irrevocable trust, is considered a resource. Also, any payment to or for the benefit of an intended beneficiary from any of these types trusts is income for Medicaid eligibility purposes. So, generally, trusts are not helpful for government benefits disability planning. An exception is a statutory special needs trust.

A statutory "supplemental care" special needs trust that meets certain requirements permits a person to enjoy a standard of living that is higher than the basic standard ordinarily provided by Medicaid, while receiving Medicaid and possibly SSI benefits. Trust assets are used to purchase things that enhance lifestyle, such as a vehicle, a TV or personal services. Because Medicaid is a joint federal/state program that is administered by the states, similar to nursing home care, each state will have its own requirements with respect to a special needs trust.

Two very common statutory special needs trusts are the (d)(4)(A) trust and the (d)(4)(C) trust. The names refers to their subparts under 42 U.S.C. §1396p. A (d)(4)(A) trust is sometimes called a first-party special needs trust. A (d)(4)(C) trust is often called a pooled trust. These trusts allow for government Medicaid benefits to be available for the disabled person, with the trust providing supplemental benefits to provide a better lifestyle. A (d)(4)(C) trust is common when there are insufficient assets to justify the cost involved with a (d)(4)(A) trust.

With respect to both a self-funded (d)(4)(A) trust and a (d)(4)(C) trust, the beneficiary must be disabled within the meaning of 42 U.S.C. §1382c(a)(3). To be so, the beneficiary must be unable to engage in any substantial gainful activity by reason of a medically determinable physical or mental impairment which can be expected to result in death or which has lasted or can be expected to last for a continuous period of not less than twelve months. Because a large asset receipt would ordinarily disqualify a Medicaid beneficiary from eligibility, some case law exists holding attorneys who settle personal injury cases without establishing a (d)(4)(A) trust liable for financial loss due to the failure. A (d)(4)(A) trust is generally considered to be a grantor trust for income tax purposes, with the beneficiary subject to income tax on the trust's annual income.

Ordinarily, a (d)(4)(A) trust is created for the benefit of a disabled person under age 65 by the disabled person, a parent, grandparent, legal guardian or a court. The assets of the disabled person are the funding source of the trust.

An asset of the trust could potentially produce income after the beneficiary attains age 65. Many of these trusts are created as a result of a settlement of a lawsuit relating to an incident that caused the disability. A self-funded trust must be irrevocable. If the assets are funded by the beneficiary, any assets remaining in the trust upon the death of the beneficiary must be paid to the state to the extent necessary to reimburse the state for medical assistance paid by the state on the trust beneficiary's behalf. In Georgia, interest is not charged.

A (d)(4)(C) pooled trust contains assets contributed by ordinarily unrelated disabled persons. At least under federal law, there is no age 65 limit. The beneficiaries are the disabled persons. Their benefits are housed in separate accounts. In this regard, it is somewhat like a 401(k) plan. Assets are pooled and invested by a nonprofit association. Assets are used to provide benefits. To the extent that amounts remaining in a beneficiary's account upon death of the beneficiary are not retained by the trust, they must be paid to the state in an amount equal to the total medical assistance paid on behalf of the beneficiary. Again, in Georgia, interest is not charged.

Another type of special needs trust is a third-party special needs trust. It is established by a person or persons other than the disabled person, using assets of the grantor(s). There is more flexibility with such a trust than there is with a (d)(4)(A) trust or a (d)(4)(C) trust. The trust terms provide for benefits for the disabled person, without causing disqualification for public benefits. Upon the death of the disabled person, remaining assets in the trust need not be paid to the state or federal government; they can be paid to any beneficiary.

ABLE Act. Originally enacted in late 2014, the Achieving a Better Life Experience (ABLE) Act created

Internal Revenue Code §529A to authorize tax-free accounts to help certain disabled persons. (A problem with a (d)(4)(A) trust is its income is not tax-exempt for income tax purposes.) The disabled person must have become disabled (including being blind) before attaining age 26. Contributions are not tax-deductible, but distributions used to help a disabled person in certain ways are not income and do not negatively impact the disabled person's eligibility for Medicaid or many other benefits. SSI benefits are potentially suspended if the account balance exceeds $100,000.

For 2019, no more than $15,000 can be contributed to a 529A account. If multiple contributors exist, the total 2019 contribution limit remains $15,000. (The limit is annual.) Generally, an amount can be rolled tax-free from a 529 account to an ABLE care account, but the rollover counts towards the annual limit. Potential uses of the funds include education, medical and dental care, employment training, housing, transportation, funeral expenses, financial management and legal fees. Each contribution potentially qualifies for the annual exclusion for gifts ($15,000 for 2019). Under the Tax Cuts and Jobs Act (of 2017), in addition to the $15,000, the beneficiary can contribute the lesser of his or her compensation for the year and the federal poverty level for a one-person household for the preceding year ($12,490 for 2019).

Distributions taken for purposes other than the personal needs of the beneficiary are subject to tax and a ten percent (10%) penalty to the extent the distributions are comprised of income. (Any distribution is prorated between total contributions and income under Internal Revenue Code section 72.) Generally, the state is entitled to whatever is in the account upon death, to the extent the state is out-of-pocket for Medicaid expenses incurred since formation of the account. Similar to 529 accounts, each state must establish its own system of accounts. An account can be established outside the individual's state of residence. Most states now have an ABLE system.

Deeming Waiver (Katie Beckett) Aid. The Katie Becket deeming waiver is a type of Medicaid that helps cover the costs of medical treatment and therapeutic services for children with physical or developmental disabilities (including retarded children). Because it is supplied by Medicaid, state laws determine eligibility, subject to overriding federal law requirements. It is helpful to families who make too much money to receive financially-based Medicaid. The parents' income in not considered when making the analysis. If the child qualifies, the child continues to reside at home with the parents, and the child receives aid from health care workers who come to the house. To be eligible in Georgia, the child's physician must certify that it is appropriate to provide care for the child at home and the estimated cost of caring for the child at home must not exceed the estimated cost of treating the child in an institution.

Other Medicaid. There are many other Medicaid benefits potentially available other than those mentioned above and elsewhere in this book. Each state's laws differ with respect to what is available. Also, other federal benefits exist. Elder care lawyers typically are very knowledgeable about Medicaid options.

Veterans' Benefits. Veterans are entitled to benefits outside the Medicaid and Social Security benefits described above. To receive pension benefits, ordinarily, a veteran must have served at least 90 days during wartime. Spousal survivor benefits are also available. If someone is a veteran or the surviving spouse of a veteran, the veterans' benefits rules should be checked for coordination with Medicaid and Social Security. Attorneys exist who have tremendous knowledge about these benefits.

Employee Benefit Plans and Subrogation. If an employee is injured in an accident, and the employee is covered by a health care plan provided by his employer, part or all of any lawsuit recovery may need to be paid to the employer or insurer to reimburse medical expenses incurred. Plan rules generally control, but state insurance laws (if applicable) might override plan terms. If such a situation exists (i.e. injury covered by an employee benefit plan), up-front planning should be undertaken to determine what can be done to maximize recovery of loss for the injured employee while not jeopardizing public benefits.

Chapter 11

Entitlements

In order to be able to effectively plan, it is necessary to have a basic understanding of our nation's entitlements systems. Sounds boring? A general summary, with pain minimization attempted, exists below. In large part because of the many exceptions, exemptions and complexities of the system, individual research should be undertaken with respect to any particular transaction.

While this topic could possibly be even more boring than the tax discussion of in Chapter 5, it is important to know if one wishes to be able to effectively plan. This is so because middle income and some upper middle income persons and households can potentially benefit from certain entitlements. If you already understand the federal entitlements system, it would probably be best for you to skip this Chapter. Much of the material of this chapter was largely taken from *Why Work? How the Federal Tax and Entitlements System Equalize Income and Wealth*, by Jonathan Godbey and Allen Buckley (2014).

Below are listed the primary federal and certain state entitlements that impact a large percent of the American population. There are many other entitlements under the federal umbrella. The system is extremely complex. In this regard, the *Congressional Research Service* noted the following in a January 31, 2011 publication by Karen Spar titled "Federal Benefits and Services for People with Low Income: Programs, Policy, and Spending, FY2008-FY2009":

- It is important to note that the definitions of countable income also vary. Some programs have explicit rules for counting income while many do not....[R]eaders should know there may be differences between programs, so that income counted in determining eligibility for one program might not be counted in another, even though the programs might appear to use similar eligibility criteria.

- Benefits provided under means-tested programs often—but not always—are excluded from the definition of income when determining eligibility for another means-tested program.

- Moreover, income (and assets, as discussed below), used to determine *eligibility* for a particular program might be evaluated differently when determining *benefit levels* under that program. Individuals with the same amount of countable income or assets might qualify for different levels of benefits, because of the program's specific calculation rules.

It should be noted that many tax credits essentially work as entitlements. Thus, a review of them in Chapter 5 might be helpful.

The anticipated growth of entitlements may place our nation's ability to survive at risk. For 2018, entitlements accounted for 61 percent of federal spending. Discretionary spending accounted for 31 percent of spending. The other 8 percent was interest expense. The entitlements' percent is anticipated to grow substantially over the coming years. According to the CBO, Medicare and Social Security then comprised approximately 75 percent of entitlements spending. President Trump's 2020 budget calls for 67 percent mandatory spending (i.e. on entitlements).

Household standard of living produced by working (i.e. take home pay, minus taxes, plus entitlements and refundable tax credits) generally increases as income increases. The following graph from 2014 shows the effective take home pay for a family of four. Effective take-home pay means the amount the family would have for a year based on a given level of earnings if all entitlements other than Medicaid and tax credits were paid in cash. An annual family income of $10,000 is complemented with entitlements and tax credits (exclusive of Medicaid), bringing the family's effective take home pay to $33,446. If total earnings increased to $25,000, the $15,000 pay increase resulted in effective take home pay increasing by $15,572 to $49,018. The marginal tax rate was negative 3.8 percent.

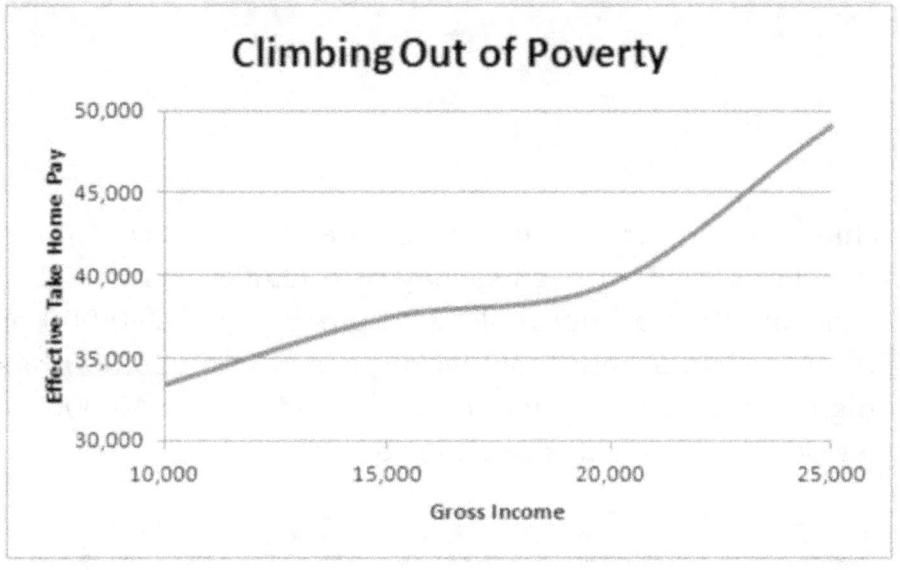

While it would likely make more sense if the above line was straight, the general upward path is presumably desirable. Charities aid lower income households, as well.

The Ditch.   While the above chart is logical, things start to fall apart for income above a certain level. For some households, standard of living diminishes as gross pay increases. The following graph shows the financial figures of a four person household stuck in "The Ditch"—an area where standard of living actually diminishes for people climbing out of poverty toward median income. As the family unit increases its pay, entitlements and tax credits decrease and effective take home pay decreases.

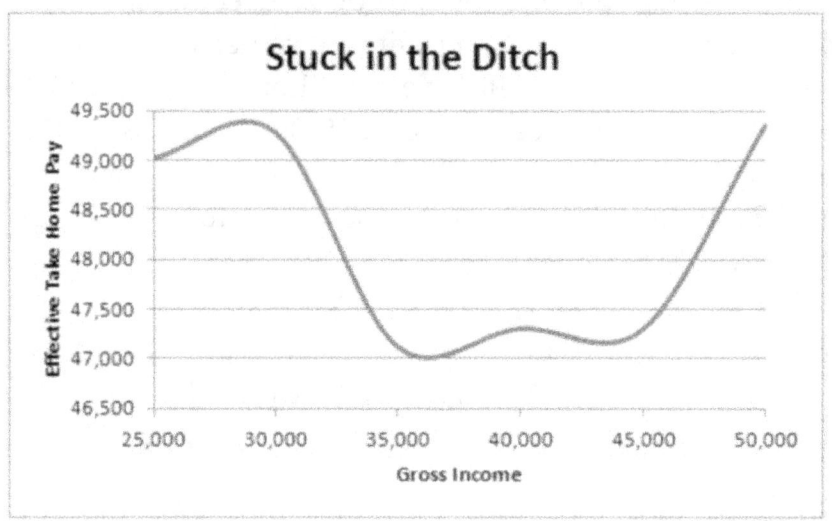

A chart showing the numbers for The Ditch follows. Note that a household with gross pay of $30,000 has a higher net income than a household with gross pay of $40,000 or $50,000. Also, a household with gross pay of $20,000 has a higher net income than a household with $40,000 of gross pay. (College aid is not considered.)

Net Income for a Family of Four with ACA Medicaid Expansion									
Gross pay	10,000	20,000	30,000	40,000	50,000	60,000	70,000	80,000	90,000	100,000
FICA	765	1,530	2,295	3,060	3,825	4,590	5,355	6,120	6,885	7,650
Federal income tax	0	0	221	1,223	2,441	3,941	5,441	6,941	8,441	9,941
EIC & child credit	-5,060	-7,372	-5,865	-3,759	-2,000	-2,000	-2,000	-2,000	-2,000	-2,000
State tax	0	69	559	1,159	1,759	2,359	2,959	3,559	4,159	4,759
Net after tax	14,295	25,773	32,790	38,317	43,975	51,110	58,245	65,380	72,515	79,650
Health Care	0	0	0	11,178	11,178	11,178	11,178	11,178	11,178	11,178
ACA Credit	0	0	0	9,213	7,813	6,265	4,584	3,578	2,628	0
Net after ACA	14,295	25,773	32,790	36,352	40,610	46,197	51,651	57,780	63,965	68,472
Housing Rent	2,568	5,568	8,568	13,200	13,200	13,200	13,200	13,200	13,200	13,200
School meals	0	0	0	252	1,278	1,278	1,278	1,278	1,278	1,278
Food at home	2,307	4,707	7,107	8,799	8,799	8,799	8,799	8,799	8,799	8,799
Cell phone	0	0	0	420	420	420	420	420	420	420
Utilities	2,070	2,070	2,070	2,070	2,400	2,400	2,400	2,400	2,400	2,400
Net income	7,350	13,428	15,045	11,611	14,513	20,100	25,554	31,683	37,868	42,375

It would seem that The Ditch was not intended by Congress, but instead came about due to the complexity of the entitlements system, when combined with the tax system. In any event, it exists.

The two largest entitlements, in terms of federal spending, are Social Security and Medicare.

Social Security — Social Security is the largest entitlement program of the federal government. It is an involuntary pension system. Social Security is also a "pay as you go system," whereby current beneficiaries receive their benefits from Social Security taxes paid by current workers. Substantially all the benefits are currently funded by payroll taxes. The tax rate is 6.2 percent of wages, and it applies to both employer and employee, up to the Social Security Wage Base in any given year. For 2019, the Social Security Wage Base is $132,900. For self-employed persons in 2019, the tax rate is 12.4 percent, and it applies to self-employment income up to $132,900. According to the Congressional Budget Office, Social Security outlays for 2018 were $982 billion.

For decades beginning in the 1980s, Social Security ran surpluses. The surpluses were loaned to the General Fund. Thus, there is a theoretical surplus of approximately $2.8 trillion in the Social Security trust fund. However, there are no hard assets that secure this fund. Rather, the fund merely possesses promissory notes from the General Fund in the form of Treasury Bills. In the future, the IOUs will need to be repaid from taxes or more debt. (When insufficient funds exist to cover benefits, the Treasury Bills are either sold on the market or redeemed. Either way, more public federal debt exists.)

Since 2010, total annual outlays have exceeded annual tax inflows. Due to the growing number of baby boomer retirements, future revenue is not expected to ever exceed future expenditures. The ratio of workers to retirees is expected to slowly decline. By approximately 2034, total revenue is expected to cover only 79 percent of expected expenditures, with a gradual reduction to 74 percent by 2092.

As explained in Chapter 9, from a benefits perspective, Social Security is very progressive. The current formula is provided at www.socialsecurity.gov. Basically, each person grows his or her annual earnings by an inflation factor and then uses the 35 years with the highest amount of "indexed earnings" to compute the benefit. The "high 35" years of indexed earnings is divided by 420 to produce average monthly indexed earnings. For 2019, this figure is then subjected to the following formula to produce the normal/full retirement age benefit: (a) the first $926 is multiplied by .9; (b) the next $4,557 is multiplied by .32; and (c) the amount in excess of $5,583 is multiplied by .15.

There are many different complex twists and turns with respect to benefits available to married persons. State law determines marriage, and federal law provides that gay persons have a right to be married. The potential combinations of benefits available to married persons are beyond the scope of this book. But, thorough analysis of options would be prudent for those approaching Social Security retirement age.

Social Security also provides disability benefits. While these benefits are beyond the scope of this text, abuses of the disability program in recent years have been well documented. Like the regular Social Security trust fund, the disability trust fund does not have sufficient asset to cover all future benefits. As of 2017, it was anticipated to be insolvent in 2028. So, combined, the Social Security old age and the Social Security disability trust funds are expected to be insolvent in 2034.

According to a September 2017 article by William R. Morton and Wayne Liou of the *Congressional Research Service* titled "Social Security: What Would happen If the Trust Funds Ran Out?," aside from the benefits cuts mentioned above, a tax increase on employer and employee from 6.2 percent to 8.0 percent would prevent a benefits cut in 2034. However, the tax would need to gradually increase to 8.45 percent by 2091. Alternatively, the rate could be fixed at 8.19 percent apiece beginning in 2034 to provide for solvency over 75 years. When Social Security last experienced insolvency (in 1983), taxes were increased and the normal retirement age was gradually increased.

Medicare — Medicare is a partially voluntary, partially involuntary health care system for retirees. A dedicated tax exists equal to 1.45 percent of compensation on employer and employee (2.9 percent of self-employment income for self-employed persons) to fund Part A of Medicare (hospitals, hospice, home health and skilled nursing facility care). Unlike Social Security, there is no cap on compensation (or self-employment income) subject to the tax. Practically, most of the remainder of Medicare is funded through the General Fund (and through general tax revenues). Due to the retirement of the baby boomers and the constantly increasing cost of health care at a rate greater than the ordinary inflation rate, Medicare is growing at a much greater rate than Social Security.

Unlike Social Security, the Medicare normal retirement age is 65. Failure to sign-up when immediately eligible can result in later large increases in required premiums.

For a hospital stay, Part A has a $1,364 deductible for 2019. After it is paid (e.g. for a hospital stay), there is no coinsurance for the first 60 days of stay. For days 61-90, coinsurance (required of the beneficiary) is $341 per day.

After day 90, the coinsurance amount increases to $682 per day for the next 60 days, assuming "lifetime reserve" days are used. No coverage exists thereafter. Different charges apply to a stay at a skilled nursing facility.

Part B of Medicare mainly covers doctor visits, outpatient care, supplies, equipment, certain home health services, procedures, and tests. Preventative services are generally covered. Technically, there is a Part B trust fund. Practically, the benefits are supplied by premiums paid by beneficiaries and the General Fund. Beneficiaries generally also pay a small portion of the Medicare-approved cost for services, procedures, and the like. An annual deductible applies ($185 for 2019), after which beneficiaries generally pay 20 percent of the costs of the Medicare-approved cost of care.

The Part B standard monthly premium for 2019 is $135.50. Some pay less. For 2019, the premium amount is greater for single people with MAGI in excess of $85,000 and for married persons who file a joint return with MAGI in excess of $170,000. The highest premium for 2019 is $460.50. It applies to single persons with MAGI above $500,000 in 2019 and married persons who file a joint return and have MAGI in excess of $750,000 in 2019.

Part C of Medicare is coverage through HMOs and private insurance preferred provider organizations (PPOs). It is similar to coverage supplied by many employers. Basically, the federal government and the beneficiary pay the cost of coverage.

Part D of Medicare relates to prescription drugs. It is partially paid for by individuals who participate. Part D was added in 2003. Obamacare significantly expanded Part D coverage. The average Part D base monthly premium for 2019 is roughly $33.50. It is higher for higher income persons. Many lower income persons qualify for free Medicare Part D coverage.

The Part D 2019 deductible is $415. The beneficiary then pays 25 percent of the cost until total costs hit $3,820, as which point the beneficiary pays all until the total paid by the beneficiary hits $5,100. (This should happen when total costs are $7,508.75.) Once drug outlays paid by the beneficiary exceed $5,100 (for 2019), catastrophic coverage kicks in, and the beneficiary need pay only the greater of five percent (5%) of a drug's cost or: (a) $3.40 for each generic drug; and (b) $8.50 for a name-brand drug. Also as to the donut hole, wherein the beneficiary pays for 100 percent of coverage, a 75 percent discount exists on brand name drugs.

Net of receipts, the Medicare costs for 2017 were $597 billion. Also for the 2017 fiscal year, the total cost for all federal health care (including Medicare, Medicaid, CHIP, ACA premium subsidies, etc.) was approximately $1 trillion. Per the Congressional Budget Office, Medicare spending for 2018 was $704 billion.

Obamacare Cost Sharing Subsidies — Obamacare provided for cost sharing subsidies to reduce the costs of health care of individuals and families with income between 100 percent and 250 percent of the FPL. Silver coverage must have been elected through the Exchange in order for these benefits to have been available. (Silver coverage does not need to be elected to receive premium credits.) The subsidies decreased as income increased. The subsidies were to cover part of deductibles, co-insurance and co-pays, to reduce the out-of-pocket costs of health care. The subsidies were designed to reduce the actuarial cost of health care (i.e. the average amount anticipated to be spent, using actuarial principles) to each covered person or household. For household income equal to or greater than to 100 percent of the FPL but not in excess of 150 percent of the FPL, the actuarial coverage percent was 94. For household income greater than 150 of the FPL but not in excess of 200 percent of the FPL, the actuarial coverage percent was 87. For household income greater than 200 percent of the FPL but not in excess of 250 percent of the FLP, the actuarial coverage percent was 73. Thus, for example, for a household with income equal to 125 percent of the FPL, the expected out-of-pocket cost for health care was to be six percent of the total costs.

As noted in Chapter 6, according to a December 27, 2018 *healthinsurance.org* article by Louise Norris, the Trump Administration stopped funding cost sharing subsidies in the fall of 2017. Insurers kept what the insured have to pay out-of-pocket for deductibles and co-pays constant, and added the cost (of covering part or all of deductibles and co-pays) to the premiums, thus making silver coverage disproportionately expensive. Since the ACA establishes premium credits by setting the maximum people must pay, and premium credits are based on a benchmark silver plan, the net effect has been increased premium credits for silver coverage. Ms. Norris noted: "This continues to be the case in 2019, and disproportionately large premium subsidies are even more widespread for 2019 than they were for 2018." The article then notes that because such subsidies are so large, some enrollees can get bronze coverage for free, or gold coverage for less than the cost of silver coverage.

For American Indians who are enrolled in any qualified health plan in the individual market through an Obamacare exchange, there must be no cost sharing whatsoever if household income does not exceed 300 percent of the FPL. This perk is one of a *tremendous* number of special entitlements available only to Indians.

For this purpose, Indians are persons who are members of an Indian tribe that is recognized as eligible for special programs and services under the U.S. Code (Title 25, Section 450b).

CHIP — The State Children's Health Insurance Program (CHIP or SCHIP) was enacted by Congress in 1997 to provide greater funding for health care for lower-income persons—to benefit children. It has been expanded by Congress. Basically, states were given the option to increase the Medicaid income coverage level or provide a new, separate insurance program. Most states increased the income coverage level to two times the FPL. Georgia adopted Peachcare, which supplies low-cost health care coverage to children who live in families not eligible for Medicaid but whose household income does not exceed 235 percent of the FPL. Federal CHIP costs for 2017 totaled approximately $16 billion.

Housing (Section 8) — Generally speaking, to qualify, household income must be 50 percent or less of the median income in the applicable county or metropolitan area. Local public housing agencies (PHAs) run the program. Vouchers are provided to eligible persons. A PHA must provide 75 percent of newly available vouchers to persons whose income does not exceed 30 percent of the median income amount for the area. Once eligible, eligibility remains until income exceeds 80 percent of the median income level for the area. So, once a person or household is eligible, there's a lot of leeway to earn more without losing the benefit. PHAs can set parameters on who is preferred for various reasons based on needs. An explanation of this program is provided at www.portal.hud.gov.

Generally, an eligible family unit must spend 30 percent of its adjusted income on rent. HUD pays the balance, and it generally pays it directly to the landlord.

The PHA determines whether a particular rental property meets HUD's standards. It also determines if rent is in line. If not, the property can still be rented, but the tenant must pay the excess of the rental amount over the amount the PHA deems reasonable. However, a family cannot pay more than 40 percent of adjusted monthly income on rent. Generally, adjusted income is annual income (i.e. wages, salary, and nonmonetary income) minus an allowance of $480 per dependent family member. However, other deductions can further reduce adjusted monthly income. A utility allowance might also apply.

Many eligible persons don't receive the benefit. Regarding the definition of "income," all cash benefits, including unemployment compensation and Social Security (regardless of taxability), are counted. Financial aid for college is excluded. Most noncash forms of assistance are not counted. An adjustment (deduction) is available for child care expenses incurred to permit a household unit member to work or go to school. (This figure can be significant.) Section 8 vouchers cost the federal government $20 billion in 2018. The program is popular, and people wait in line to get the vouchers.

Utilities — LIHEAP (low-income home energy assistance program) provides utilities cost relief to low-income persons. The states administer it. In Georgia, the 2017 annual amount was either $310 or $350. Households with income below 60 percent of the state's median income (based on family size) qualify. For 2017, the cutoffs for Georgia were $21,881, $28,614, $35,346, $42,079, $48,812, and $55,544 for families of one, two, three, four, five and six people, respectively. Federal funding of LIHEAP cost the federal government approximately $4 billion in 2018.

College — Federal financial aid for college was thoroughly summarized in Chapter 7. Education tax credits are discussed in Chapter 5.

TANF — TANF stands for Temporary Assistance for Needy Families. It is welfare. While welfare was prevalent prior to significant reforms in the 1990s, in recent years, the prevalence of traditional welfare has diminished substantially. However, the other entitlements discussed herein, including SNAP (food stamps), have been greatly expanded in recent years. The Georgia Department of Human Services (DHS) website notes that there were 3,442 adults receiving TANF benefits in 2011, and the total case number was then 19,256. TANF cost the federal government approximately $16 billion in 2018.

Medicaid — As previously noted, the U.S. Supreme Court decision of 2012 regarding the constitutionality of Obamacare permitted states to reject ACA's income expansion requirement of Medicaid to 138 percent of the FPL. ACA originally required the expansion, and federal law generally provides that a state must do what the federal government says in order to receive the federal Medicaid funds. The Supreme Court ruled that a state's (continued) receipt of Medicaid funding could not be conditioned on its expansion. Those states that did not expand in the initial years did not receive federal funding that would have fully covered the expansion. Note: The "Subsidy Calculator" of the Kaiser Family Foundation website (http://kff.org/interactive/subsidy-calculator/) was used to provide virtually all of the Obamacare premiums and premium tax credit figures produced in this book. (The zip code generally used was 30126.)

Many states have done something short of ACA's anticipated expansion of Medicaid. Like many states, Georgia has (as of January of 2019) rejected Obamacare's

Medicaid expansion. Georgia residents who are either citizens or lawful residents potentially qualify for certain benefits that are not quite as generous as those provided by Obamacare. Eligibility is confirmed semiannually. For 2017, federal and state spending on Medicaid totaled $582 billion. According to the Congressional Budget Office, Medicaid cost the federal government $389 billion in 2018, and is anticipated to cost $406 billion in 2019.

SSI — Supplemental Security Income (SSI) is provided to disabled, blind and age 65 or older persons or couples who have little income. SSI is funded by general tax revenue, and it is administered by the Social Security Administration. Blind or disabled children can also qualify. For 2019, SSI supplements "countable income" so as to increase monthly income to $771 for single persons and $1,157 for couples. For 2018, SSI cost to the federal government was $55 billion.

Head Start — The Head Start program essentially offers preschool and related nutrition and dental services. It is available to children in families whose income level does not exceed the FPL. Families whose income does not exceed 130 percent of the FPL can also potentially qualify. In 2017, Head Start cost the federal government $9 billion.

Voluntary Medicare Prescription Drug Benefit — This entitlement is available to seniors and people with disabilities. Non-disabled seniors with incomes no higher than 150 percent of the FPL potentially qualify. Essentially, no Medicare Part D premiums need be paid.

Lifeline cell phone — Lifeline entitles the beneficiary to a free cell phone and 250 minutes of cell phone use each month. Additional minutes can be purchased for very little cost. To participate, income must not exceed 135 percent of FPL or the person must be eligible for any one of the following programs: Medicaid, SNAP, SSI, Section 8 housing, or one or more of a few other programs. The FPL is based on family size. Income generally includes ordinary cash inflow.

One phone is allowed per family. A recent study showed that ninety-two percent of lower-income households receive the benefit. The funding source is the Federal Universal Service Fund, which is funded by fees charged to people who use phones and pay for service plans. Often, the fees are listed as a separate line item on a phone bill.

Food —Similar to health care, a variety of programs provide food. Under the Child and Adult Care Food Program (CACFP), children under age 12 and elderly adults are eligible for free meals and snacks if their income is below 130 percent of the FPL. (Higher figures apply to Alaska and Hawaii.) Reduced-cost meals and snacks are available if income does not exceed 185 percent of the FPL. (Higher figures apply to Alaska and Hawaii.)

The Supplemental Nutrition Assistance Program (SNAP) provides food stamp-type benefits. In 2019, 38 million Americans are expected to receive SNAP benefits. Households must not have countable assets in excess of $2,250 if under age 60, or $3,500 if over age 59. Home value is excluded. Generally, retirement plan and IRA assets are also excluded. In most states, the value of vehicles is excluded.

Generally, non-disabled persons between age 16 and 60 must either work, register for work, accept suitable employment if offered and not voluntarily quit, or participate in training programs for work to be eligible. While retirement plan assets are excluded from the assets calculations, the income from such a plan (or from an IRA) is counted for purposes of the income test. Income that is counted includes all traditional taxable income, including pensions and unemployment compensation. Excluded from income are noncash income, housing subsidies, education assistance, and certain "irregular income."

Gross and net income tests apply for SNAP benefits. However, elderly persons and disabled persons need only meet a net income test. Under the gross income test, gross income of the family unit cannot exceed 130 percent of the FPL. Under the net income test, net income cannot exceed the FPL. Figures are calculated monthly. The following monthly deductions are permitted for 2019: 20 percent of earned income, a standard deduction of $164 for a family size of one to three people and $174 for a family of four, dependent care expenses when needed for work or for going to school, child support payments, and an "excess shelter" deduction. (Higher standard deductions are available for families with more than four persons, and for people living in Alaska or Hawaii.) Maximum monthly allotments exist. For 2019 for a family of four, it is $642. The excess shelter deduction is available if more than half of a household's income is used to pay utilities, phone, rent or mortgage payments and taxes on a home. The deduction (which is the excess amount) is limited to $552. The monthly net income is multiplied by 0.3 to produce the required contribution of the family. There are fixed "allotments" of benefits, from which the family's required contribution is deducted to produce the monthly benefit. The maximum monthly allotments are $192, $353, $505, $642, $762, $914, $1,011 and $1,155 for families of one to eight members. An additional $144 of allotment per member is permitted for families with more than eight members. In 2019, SNAP is expected to cost the federal government $58 billion.

WIC — The Special Supplemental Nutrition Program for Women, Infants, and Children (WIC) provides benefits to low-income women, infants, and children. Women generally qualify while pregnant and up to six weeks after giving birth. Infants qualify up until their first birthday. Children qualify up until age 5. Basically, WIC provides free healthy food to people who are potentially subject to nutrition risk. A physician or nurse must determine whether the person is eligible. To be eligible, income must not exceed 185 percent of the FPL. However, people receiving Medicaid, SNAP, or TANF automatically qualify. Fifty-three percent of U.S. infants receive WIC benefits. In 2018, WIC costs totaled approximately $6 billion.

The Commodity Supplemental Food Program (CSFP) — The CSFP provides free food to pregnant and breastfeeding women, infants, children up to age 6, and persons age 60 or older. The USDA purchases food and provides it to state agencies for distribution at centers. Generally, family income for elderly persons must be at or below 130 percent of the FPL. For women, infants, and children, the income level generally is 185 percent of the FPL. Women, infants, and children who receive Medicaid, SNAP, or TANF benefits are automatically eligible. *However*, only women, infants and children who applied to participate in CSFP prior to February 7, 2014 are eligible. Women cannot participate in both WIC and CSFP.

School breakfast program (SBP) — Under the SBP, children from families with household income at or below 130 percent of the FPL are eligible for free breakfasts at school. For children whose family income is between 130 and 185 percent of the FPL, the student is entitled to low-cost breakfasts. For these meals, the charge for a low-cost breakfast cannot be more than 30 cents. The USDA provides the cash for the program. In the 2016 fiscal year, 14.6 million children received a free or reduced-cost lunch. For 2017, SBP cost the federal government $4 billion.

School lunch program (SLP) —The eligibility standards for the SLP are the same as those for the SBP. The lunch cost for those children whose families fall in the 130–185 percent range cannot exceed 40 cents. Schools can also qualify for "bonus" USDA foods when they are available from surplus agricultural stocks. For 2017, the SLP cost the federal government $14 billion.

Chapter 12

Common Scenarios and Decision-Making

Common Scenarios

Individuals and households will generally fall within a few scenarios with respect to ongoing run-of-the mill planning. The most common are mentioned below. Obviously, many individuals and households will have their own twists, etc., that could justify doing something different. Importantly, the general year-to-year guidance supplied below assumes the current system, or something very similar to it, will remain intact. It also assumes that system won't "collapse" due to excess federal debt, etc. For the reasons set forth in Chapter 1, such an assumption might not be reasonable. However, choices need to be made, and in terms of politics, there ordinarily is safety in numbers.

Single With Full-Time Job and Without Self-Employment Option. This category of person is someone who works one job as an employee and either wants to work only one job or, practically, can work only one job. Such a person would ordinarily want to do certain things to maximize his or her financial outcome.

Because the person is not self-employed, creation of a personal retirement plan is not an option. If a retirement plan exists at work, it very likely is a 401(k) plan (or a 403(b) or 457(b) plan). Absent a dire need for cash, the individual should contribute substantially to the employer plan. (If the plan has a loan feature, it can help in a short-term cash squeeze.) Assuming matching contributions are provided, and the matching contributions are or will become vested, contributions should ordinarily at least be sufficient to capture the maximum matching contributions.

While considering investments held outside the employer's 401(k) plan, total investments should be substantially diversified, with special attention to long-term bonds and investments potentially holding them (including possibly target date funds).

If the employer maintains a cafeteria plan (as many employers and most large employers do), participation should be undertaken if one or more of the benefits offered is needed. Anything chosen other than cash is wholly or partially nontaxable. Thus, it would be prudent to purchase something needed through a cafeteria plan when its purchase reduces taxes.

If affordable minimum essential coverage is not offered by the employer, the person should consider purchasing healthcare via the ACA exchange. Chapter 6 provides details.

If the person anticipates an income change in the following year, and also does not anticipate significant tax system changes, income should be either deferred or accelerated, as feasible, and deductions should be reasonably accelerated or deferred, as feasible. Specifics and examples are provided in Chapter 5.

If a permanent home is desired, purchasing such can produce significant tax benefits, primarily tax-deductibility of mortgage interest payments as itemized deductions and (generally) tax-free sales. For many, the higher standard deduction created by TCJA will make itemizing deductions not worthwhile. Some entitlement benefits also exist. However, care should be taken so that a home purchase does not take place during a housing bubble, or when mortgage rates are relatively high. At the beginning of 2019, mortgage rates were relatively low.

Married With Full-Time Job(s) and Without Self-Employment Option. This category of persons is a married couple with respect to which: (a) one or both of the couple works one job as an employee; and (b) neither of the couple can and wants to work another job or be self-employed. The things the couple would want to do to maximize their financial outcome are identical or very similar to the things the single person described above would want to do. Thus, 401(k) contributions should be prudently and consistently made, cafeteria plan participation should be undertaken if benefits are desired (and the employer maintains a plan), and year-end tax planning outlined in Chapter 5 should be undertaken annually. If a permanent home is desired, ordinarily, one should be purchased.

Single with Full-Time Job and Self-Employment Option. For this person, a self-employment option exists with the person *not* being a partner with another person (through a partnership, LLC, corporation, etc.). If the decision is made to undertake self-employment outside the regular job, numerous possibilities become available in terms of tax planning. First, the proper choice of business entity should be undertaken. The various options are discussed in Chapter 4. For reasons set forth in Chapter 4, most people will want to form a single member LLC through which to conduct their self-employment business. For some, an S election would make sense.

A self-employed person can establish his or her own retirement plan. It can be crafted to fit the person's age and financial situation. Younger people and people not making a lot of money will likely wish to establish a 401(k)/profit sharing plan. Here, it should be kept in mind that the annual 401(k) contribution limit (for 2019: $19,000 or $25,000 if 50+) applies to all 401(k) plans with respect to which an individual is eligible on a combined basis. Since the employer's plan provides employer-funded matching contributions, it would be prudent to contribute at least the amount necessary to maximize matching contributions to the employer's 401(k) plan. An individual who "maxes out" under his employer's 401(k) plan (and receives the maximum employer-funded matching contributions) could make only profit sharing contribution to the plan of his self-employed business. (A 25 percent of plan compensation limit would ordinarily apply.)

Older, relatively wealthier persons would likely be best suited by establishing a cash balance plan or other pension plan. If consistency of cash flows is an issue, the cash balance plan might have an allocation formula that provides lesser benefits for pay (including self-employment earnings) below a certain threshold (e.g. 10 percent up to $50,000) and greater benefits for pay above the threshold (e.g. 60 percent of annual compensation in excess of $50,000). If an S election is made for the business, it is possible to pay relatively little compensation early in the year, and then make a large bonus payment later in the year, so as to produce desired plan compensation (on which benefits are based). For middle age persons, it might be best to switch to a pension plan (possibly a cash balance plan) if they have children who will enter into college in the near future, so as to minimize taxes (and health care costs, if affordable minimum essential coverage is not provided by the employer) and maximize federal financial aid for college. (See Chapters 5, 6 and 7 for details.)

If health care is not provided by the employer, the self-employed individual can ordinarily purchase it through an ACA exchange. Cafeteria plan benefits ordinarily would not be available to a single member business without employees. Such benefits should be taken advantage of through the employer's cafeteria plan, if one exists and benefit needs exist.

The other tax considerations applicable to persons without a self-employment option apply. Thus, ordinarily, it would be prudent for such a person to consistently make 401(k) contributions to the employer's plan (where matching contributions can be garnered) and undertake year-end tax planning as outlined in Chapter 5. If a permanent home is desired and the conditions are right, one should be purchased.

Married with Full-Time Job and Self-Employment Option. This category of persons is a married couple with respect to which: (a) one of the couple works one job; (b) the other of the couple does not work a job; and (c) one or both of the couple wants to work on a self-employed basis and, practically, one or both of the couple can be self-employed. The things the couple would want to do to maximize their financial outcome are very similar to the things the single person described immediately above would want to do.

A business entity should be chosen for the self-employed business. A retirement plan can be and, absent financial constraints, should be created. Health care should be purchased through ACA exchange if not available from the employer's plan and the household qualifies for ACA benefits. Contributions should be consistently made to the employer's 401(k) plan, cafeteria plan participation should be undertaken under the employer's cafeteria plan (if one exists and or more benefits are desired), and year-end tax planning outlined in Chapter 5 should be undertaken annually. If a permanent home is desired and conditions are right, one should be purchased.

Single With Full-Time Job and Co-ownership Option. This category of persons is a single person who has a full-time job and has the option to work as a member in a multiple member LLC, a partner in a partnership or a shareholder in a corporation that has other shareholders. Such a person is similarly situated to the single person who has a full-time job and can be self-employed in his own (exclusively owned) business, except the planning options are more limited due to the fact that other owners of the business exist. Only employers and self-employed persons can establish tax-qualified retirement plans. Only an employer can maintain a cafeteria plan. A business owned by more than one person will adopt only those employee benefit plans that its owners, as a group and pursuant to the overriding governance documents, choose to adopt. (For an LLC, the operating agreement typically is the governing document. For a corporation, the bylaws ordinarily are the governing document.)

Consider an LLC owned and operated by two members, one old and the other young. Assume the business has a few non-owner employees. The younger member might wish for the company to adopt a 401(k)/profit sharing plan while the older member desires for a cash balance plan to be maintained. A cash balance plan must cover the lesser of 40 percent of eligible employees or two employees (or one employee if there is only one employee). While it might be possible to establish two separate plans, one covering one member and a subset of employees and the other covering the other member and the remainder of the employees, query whether doing so would be cost-effective? Ordinarily, such is not done. As discussed in Chapter 4, whenever a business will be owned by two persons in equal shares, some sort of tie-breaker voting provision should exist.

Married With Full-Time Job and Co-ownership Option. If one of a married couple falling under second married possibility described above has the option to work as a member in a multiple member LLC, partner in a partnership or shareholder in a corporation that has other shareholders, the considerations suppled above with respect to a single person equally apply.

Estate Planning. Because of the large exemption, it is assumed that readers of this book won't be subject to the estate or gift tax. For married persons with a solid marriage who live in states where probate is not burdensome or costly (such as Georgia), "disclaimer" wills will often be the most attractive estate planning will tool. Using such a will, all assets that pass through the probate process will be inherited by the surviving spouse except to the extent the surviving spouse disclaims the right to receive assets. Assets disclaimed pass to an alternative beneficiary or beneficiaries (such as children or grandchildren) designated under the will to receive assets in the event of disclaimer. For married persons living in states where probate is burdensome or costly, the same result can be achieved by utilizing a revocable trust. Where a revocable trust is used, a pour over will should also exist. (Note: Some advisors whose clients live in states where probate is not burdensome or costly recommend using a revocable trust and pour over will.)

For single persons living in a state where probate is not burdensome or costly, a will often will be the preferred means of passing assets that pass through probate. For single persons living in a state where probate is burdensome or costly, a revocable trust coupled with a pour over will ordinarily or often be the preferred means of passing probate assets.

For persons living in states were probate is uncostly and not burdensome and who own real property in a state where probate is costly or burdensome, it likely makes sense to form a single member LLC under the laws of residence of the individual to own the property. By doing so, no probate process should come into play. The LLC membership could pass pursuant to the terms of the will of the LLC owner.

Whenever an amount is to be left to a minor or someone with financial concerns (because of the person himself or herself or a person to whom they are married, etc.), assets can be left in trust via a trust set up pursuant to the terms of a will (i.e. a testamentary trust). The trust might provide that assets are held in the trust until a certain time or times passes (such as attainment of a particular age or ages). A trustee would ordinarily be named in the will.

As noted in Chapter 5, because assets owned at death receive a "step up" in basis to fair market value (or a step down, if they have depreciated in value), it is best to place appreciated assets in the hands of someone who is near in time to death. If assets are held in a trust, it might be possible to terminate the trust and have the appreciated assets placed in the name of a beneficiary who is near death.

Decision-Making

Decisions need to be made in light of all pertinent laws and rules impacting the decision-making process. What laws and rules are pertinent will vary with the circumstances of each person or household.

For a person or household without a child or children in college or in high school, the equation will generally be different than the equation for those with a child or children in college or high school. The reason this is so is that a person or household with a child or children in college or high school will want to take federal financial aid for college into consideration, whereas for those without a child or children in college or high school will ordinarily not need or want to take college aid into consideration. Of course, if it is anticipated that a child or children will be applying for college at some point in time, planning should take that future possibility into account.

Example 1. A household has two adults and two children, one of whom is in her first year of college. One of the adults works—as a CPA, and anticipates making $125,000 in 2019. The family participates in Obamacare, and the couple ordinarily contributes substantially to retirement plans to reduce AGI in an effort to cut health care costs and taxes. Assume itemized deductions for 2019 will be less than the standard deduction of $24,400, and virtually all of the family's wealth is in the form of their home, tax-qualified plan assets, 529 accounts, and IRAs. It is December 31, 2019, and there is $1,000 of excess cash on hand. Four possible uses are considered: (1) pay 2019 estimated state tax liability of $1,000; (2) contribute $1,000 to a 529 account; (3) pay $1,000 to a 401(k) account; or (4) pay January 2020 office rent of $1,000. Which is the best option?

Unless the payment caused total itemized deductions to exceed $24,400 (unlikely), paying $1,000 for state tax liability produces no tax benefit or Obamacare benefit whatsoever. Also, it has no impact on FAFSA benefits. Similarly, using the $1,000 to fund a 529 plan produces no current tax benefit or Obamacare benefit whatsoever. Also, FAFSA benefits are unchanged. Using the $1,000 to fund a 401(k) contribution reduces AGI, thus reducing tax liability and Obamacare costs (with a 15-30 percent effective rate).

FAFSA is not impacted because 401(k) contributions are added back when doing FAFSA calculations, except the assets will not be included in family assets once in the 401(k) plan. Paying the January 2020 office rent reduces AGI and FAFSA income, thus reducing taxes, Obamacare costs and future college costs (likely at a 47 percent FAFSA rate and 15 to 30 percent taxes/Obamacare rate—combined savings of roughly $700)—it is the best alternative. *Note*: If the person was an employee instead of being self-employed and received solid health plan coverage at work, option 3 (i.e. contributing to the employer's 401(k) plan) would likely be the best option.

Example 2. Let's analyze a self-employed Georgia resident who has substantial savings but has not made significant money in the recent past. Assume the person is married and the family has two children. The spouse does not work for compensation. Also assume the household's total income for 2019 is anticipated to be $100,000, and its only component will be self-employment income. Also assume the household will make discretionary retirement contributions of $55,000, and has a $7,065 deduction for one-half of self-employment tax, reducing AGI to $37,935. As such, the household is eligible for significant Obamacare benefits. The total tax liability for 2019, without Obamacare credits and the child credits, was $15,213. After Obamacare credits and the other credits totaling $25,693, a refund of $10,480 will be due. Also assume: Net worth from investments other than home equity and retirement assets totals $150,000. The oldest parent is age 54 in 2019. Finally, as is the case for all other examples in this book, assume the tax system will remain unchanged.

Assume an opportunity exists to work more, and make more money. Three possible incremental net income possibilities are considered. In one, $30,000 of additional taxable income will be made. In the second, $60,000 of additional taxable income will be made. In the third, $90,000 of additional taxable income will be made.

Looking simply at federal and state taxes (net of credits), earning $30,000 more taxable income would increase 2019 net taxes by $9,121, meaning the net cash increase would be $20,879. The incremental rate is 30 percent. For $60,000 of additional earnings, net taxes would increase by $16,845, netting $43,155. The incremental rate is 28 percent. For $90,000, net tax would increase $42,192, netting $47,808—a 47 percent incremental rate.

Now let's assume college education is a factor, because there is a child in her freshman year of college. Assuming lowering the EFC substantially reduces the amount the family must pay for college dollar-for-dollar (which often is not the case), the results change much more dramatically.

Using the 2019-2020 FAFSA tables (which would ordinarily look back two years; here, they are used to estimate EFC two years into the future), increasing net earnings by $30,000 causes the EFC for college to increase by $10,974. Adding the tax increase of $9,121 produces a total incremental cost of $19,915, meaning only $10,085 of net cash would be received. For $60,000 of increased earnings, the EFC increases by $25,030. Adding the tax increase of $16,845 produces a total incremental cost of $41,875, meaning only $18,125 of net cash would be received. For $90,000 of increased earnings, the EFC increases by $27,329. Adding the tax increase of $41,192 produces a total incremental cost of $69,521, meaning only $20,479 of net cash would be received.

As noted in Chapter 7, it might be possible to "fix" college aid in terms of dollars received in scholarships, etc. from a college or university in year 1, thereby mitigating or eliminating the EFC part of the foregoing analysis. Also, it should be noted that not all colleges are equal and not all college aid is equal. Grants are worth much more than loans. And, some schools will cover all of the cost or virtually all of the cost of students they accept.

People need to do these analyses before they make a move. Sometimes, the incremental income can necessitate a lengthy drive to a new place of work or another form of stress. From a big picture perspective, often, it will be best not to make the extra money. The most important point is that all pertinent variables need to be considered when making such important decisions.

Example 3. Assume the year is 2019 and the family described in Example 2 is expecting a significant income increase in the next few years due to a major event, and they have substantial savings in Roth IRAs. Also assume their credit is solid, and they have access to cheap credit using credit cards. For example, assume they can borrow $10,000 for an annual fee of 2 percent, for a cost of $200. Or, they can take a penalty-free $10,000 Roth distribution. Which is the best option, given that the child (or children) in college situation?

Taking a $10,000 Roth distribution would not impact tax liability or Obamacare eligibility. This is so because the income is tax-free, and does not count for either purpose. But, a Roth distribution could result in as much as $4,700 being additionally required for college tuition and fees in 2020. So, it would ordinarily be best to borrow, pay less for college, and then later pay off the credit card debt when the income increase is realized.

www.ingramcontent.com/pod-product-compliance
Lightning Source LLC
Chambersburg PA
CBHW080956170526
45158CB00010B/2820